Speak, Move, Play and Learn with Children on the Autism Spectrum

by the same authors

Speech in Action
Interactive Activities Combining Speech Language Pathology and Adaptive Physical Education
America X Gonzalez, Lois Jean Brady and Jim Elliott
ISBN 978 1 84905 846 9

of related interest

Social Communications Cues for Young Children with Autism Spectrum Disorders and Related Conditions
How to Give Great Greetings, Pay Cool Compliments and Have Fun with Friends
Tarin Varughese
ISBN 978 1 84905 870 4

Motivate to Communicate!
300 Games and Activities for Your Child with Autism
Simone Griffin and Dianne Sandler
ISBN 978 1 84905 041 8

Challenge Me!
Speech and Communication Cards
Amanda Elliott
Illustrated by David Kemp
ISBN 978 1 84310 946 4

LOIS JEAN BRADY, AMERICA X GONZALEZ,
MACIEJ ZAWADZKI AND CORINDA PRESLEY

Illustrated by Byron Roy James

Speak, Move, Play and Learn with Children on the Autism Spectrum

Activities to Boost Communication Skills, Sensory Integration and Coordination Using Simple Ideas from Speech and Language Pathology and Occupational Therapy

Jessica Kingsley *Publishers*
London and Philadelphia

Front cover image source: Shutterstock®. The cover image is for illustrative purposes only, and any person featuring is a model.

First published in 2011
by Jessica Kingsley Publishers
116 Pentonville Road
London N1 9JB, UK
and
400 Market Street, Suite 400
Philadelphia, PA 19106, USA

www.jkp.com

Library of Congress Cataloging in Publication Data
A CIP catalog record for this book is available from the Library of Congress

British Library Cataloguing in Publication Data
Speak, move, play, and learn with children on the autism spectrum : activities to boost communication skills, sensory integration, and coordination, using simple ideas from speech and language pathology, and occupational therapy / Lois Jean Brady ... [et al.] ; illustrated by Byron Roy James.
p. cm.
Includes bibliographical references.
ISBN 978-1-84905-872-8 (alk. paper)
1. Autistic children--Rehabilitation. I. Brady, Lois Jean.
RJ506.A9S67 212
618.9285882--dc23
2011034773

ISBN 978 1 84905 872 8
eISBN 978 0 85700 531 1

Printed and bound in Great Britain

This book is dedicated to the therapists, teachers, parents, daycare providers, and support staff who never give up hope, and continue to work hard to ensure that our children have every chance available to learn the skills they will need, so that one day they will not need us any more.

CONTENTS

ACKNOWLEDGMENTS

Lois's

A huge thank you goes to America who went above and beyond the call of duty to make this book the wonderfully robust finished product that it is. Thanks a bunch to Gary who skillfully managed the household allowing me the time to get my thoughts and experiences down on paper. Thanks also to my teenagers, Ian and Stephanie, for pitching in and fixing my dinner for a change.

Big-time thank you to Rachel Menzies and all the wonderful folks at Jessica Kingsley Publishers for making this book a reality, and for all the wonderful work they do for the Special Needs community.

Last but not least, thanks Mom! My biggest cheerleader.

America's

I want to thank everyone from Jessica Kingsley Publishers for their dedication to our labor of love. I am very happy to have had the chance to work with such an imaginative, creative, and hard working individual like Lois; thanks for being my partner and friend. I would also like to thank my sister Citlalli Gonzalez for spending her time to help me when I was freaking out. Thanks to Isis Gonzalez and Rosa Zavala for their wonderful ideas when I was stumped, and to my love, Larry, who was there for me through a very rough year of losses. I send a special thank you to my mom and dad for their support throughout the years. And finally I would like to dedicate this book to my other dad, Fernando, who passed away this year and didn't get to see this book published. I love you all.

Maciej's

This book would not be possible without the open-mindedness of my students, who participated in the often difficult "trial-and-error" process of altering activities to make them better and more fun. I would like to thank all of you for your flexibility and understanding. Also, I would like to extend my gratitude to everyone who never stopped believing that this book would see the light of day and supported me during those months. Thank you, Mom.

Corinda's

Thank you God for blessing me with the opportunity to serve you in this way. Even on the most challenging of days, the kiddos I work with give me some reason to smile, either with their simple humor or with their quirky reasoning. Many, many thanks and much love to my wonderful husband, Jason, and beautiful daughter, Londyn. I would not be who I am without you. Thank you to Mom for your endless sacrifice, and thank you to Dad for showing me how to follow my passion. You always told me, "If you find something that you love to do and you're excited to get up in the morning for, you are a very lucky person." Guess I should go play the lottery.

ABOUT THE ILLUSTRATOR

Byron Roy James came into this world early, at three pounds, in a rural Russian hospital, where he stayed for his first 15 months. He was adopted by American parents, Jann and Nathan James, whom Byron made very proud and happy. Byron's talents presented themselves quickly, one of many being his artwork. His specialty was drawing in three-dimensional perspective at the age of five, without any instruction. Byron has never stopped drawing. His parents discovered his Asperger gifts and challenges early, and Byron has grown into a healthy, fun-loving, kind, talented, and very social young man. Currently, Byron is pursuing his varied interests and hobbies, including electric guitar, cooking, drawing cityscapes, studying modern transportation systems, road biking, racquetball, turtles, and just having a good time with family. He currently lives in Pleasant Hill, California, with his parents, his 13-year-old brother and sister, and a menagerie of family pets. He entered his Sophomore year of high school in the fall of 2011.

Introduction

How to use this book

This book was made with the aim of easy use in mind. It is put together in a way that enables the reader to open it at any page and find a fun activity or lesson plan that can be done with minimal materials and tons of variations to adjust to the appropriate level of the child involved. Most of the activities require materials that are readily available in the home, school, or therapy room. There are even some variations that can be done with no materials at all. The practicality of the activities was made a priority in order to reach out to busy therapists, teachers, parents, and daycare providers. In a world that seems always to be on the run and constantly rushing, a simple yet effective book can be a valuable tool in our quest for educating our young.

These lessons are meant to be shared with other members of the educational team so that they can be generalized across environments. For example, if teachers do a lesson in school, they can send a note home (or to the daycare provider) so that parents or care providers can reinforce the things taught that day. By reinforcing the lessons we can provide our children with more opportunities to practice them and increase the chances that they will remember what was taught. This sort of inter-environmental generalization promotes fluidity and connectivity.

In this book we will use terms like "teacher," "student," "child," and "group." A group can be a parent and child, or a parent and a few children, or a therapist and one or more clients. This is also true for teachers and daycare providers.

Keep in mind, however, that the term "teacher" is interchangeable for parents, daycare providers, and therapists alike. After all, anyone who teaches a lesson is a teacher even if they are also a parent. The reasoning behind this train of thought is that parents teach their children, care providers teach their students, and therapists teach their clients. We are all teachers, and we are all in this together. That is why we chose to come together to put our collaborative efforts forward in an attempt to reach out to our children in a way that inspires them to learn.

Helpful icons

The light bulb icon represents tried and true bright ideas. These smart ideas, tips, recommendations, and morsels of wisdom can help the activities run smoothly and allow the students to have a memorable learning experience. When you see the light bulb icon, take a few seconds to learn something that will benefit you as you do your activity.

The band aid represents a solution to a possible hazard. Be careful and proceed with a watchful eye. If you see this icon, be aware that there is the potential for spilling, scraping, cutting, or choking hazards. Accidents can happen anywhere at any time. We want to prevent accidents so that the activities are fun and worry free.

STOP, sit on your hands, close your eyes, and let your students make (safe) mistakes. We learn from our mistakes. Use encouragement and gentle guidance, and give extra time for problem solving. Remember that the experience is the main focus of any activity, not the end product. Allow the children to do their own work even if you feel compelled to do it for them.

Best practices and strategies that guarantee success

Best practices are evidence-based instructional approaches that yield educationally enriched results across different environments. Below are the various practices and strategies that we have found to be highly effective in supporting students to reach their educational and personal goals. Remember—know your students. A practice that has worked well for one particular student may not work for another. We have had a high level of success with students using the following strategies. It is our sincerest hope that you will too.

- Have a clear idea of what your goal for each activity is. Educators, family members, and therapists should clearly understand and commit to a common goal that fits the student's individual needs and abilities.

- Expect your students to succeed. Students can achieve their goals when standards of performance are made clear. When educators or caregivers believe that "all students can learn and I can teach them," it will lead to extraordinary results.

- At the beginning of each activity choose one or two key ingredients or materials and have the students describe them with their five senses. What does it smell like? What does it taste like? What does it look like? What does it feel like? What does it sound like? See the Appendix for a list of descriptors.

- Set up the environment so that every student succeeds and has a positive experience, while inspiring them to do their best.

- Before each activity insist on greetings, handshakes, and high fives, or saying, "Hello, good to see you."

- After each activity have a re-cap of what the students did and encourage them to share their experiences. We all do this, usually over a cup of coffee, so let's teach it.

- At the end of the session insist on a salutation appropriate for the day. For example, "Have a good weekend," "Happy holiday," "See you later."

- Let the students make mistakes and mess up. This is a valuable learning opportunity. Let them ask for help. Let them clean their messes. Do not offer to help or to fix something without the student initiating the plea.

- Replace verbal prompting with time prompts and give extra time for students to problem solve. Students with special needs may take extra time to process information. Too much prompting may interfere with learning and independence.

- Remember, the value of the activity is in the process, not always the finished product. It's OK if the final product is slightly askew. Let the nose be where the mouth belongs or the lemonade be too lemony. They will always do better the next time.

- Let them get it on their fingers. Enough said.

- Have fun.

What is *Speak, Move, Play and Learn with Children on the Autism Spectrum?*

Occupational therapists work with those who possess, or are at risk of developing, physical or cognitive disabilities, psychosocial dysfunction, developmental or learning disorders, and other disorders or conditions. Occupational therapists use tools such as sensory-motor, neuro-developmental, and visual motor and perception techniques in treatment. They adapt or alter tasks and activities to promote a person's health and wellness (American Occupational Therapy Association (AOTA) 2008). Speech and language pathologists (SLPs) or speech and language therapists (SLTs) address speech and vocal production, swallowing difficulties, and language needs through speech therapy in a variety of different settings including schools, hospitals, and private practice. They work with patients on a number of specific speech issues including intonation and prosody, articulation, content, and the facilitation of conversational skills. The activities in this book all combine tools and ideas from speech and language pathology and occupational therapy. Each field possesses a unique perspective on clients' needs and brings a specialized point of view to the treatment or education plan.

This book is brought together by speech and language pathologists and occupational therapists working in a non-public school with children with autism and other developmental disorders. These children present challenging behaviors that interfere with their daily functioning, and therefore we are sensitive to the need to structure activities so that any child can succeed. We have combined aspects of speech, assistive technology, sensory integration, and motor planning in all the activities in this book. We find that creating lesson plans with fun and exciting activities peaks our students' interest and maintains their attention.

Historically, speech and language therapists have addressed communication and language issues, while occupational therapists focus on motor and sensory integration issues. Watling *et al.* (1999) examined the current practice patterns of occupational therapists and found a high frequency of collaboration with other professionals in various therapeutic settings. They stated that 98 percent of respondents collaborated with speech therapists in school settings for both evaluation and intervention.

Speech and occupational therapists both have a responsibility to communicate and educate family members, caregivers, and others to best assist the child (AOTA 2008). Collaboration between various professional fields, as well as including parents and caregivers, appears to be the key in finding the most efficient means in helping kids with their struggles (Briesmeister and Schaefer 1998).

Why it works

Kielhofner (1992, p.15) suggested that active engagement in a variety of occupations promotes and maintains physical, cognitive, and emotional health while, conversely, lack of engagement in occupations leads to deterioration and dysfunction. We believe the blend of speech, assistive technology, and occupational therapy in meaningful activity is a productive means of facilitating learning and development. Learning is achieved through experiencing situations and interacting or reacting in a multi-sensory environment. In order to generalize learned experience to various contexts or settings, one must attach personal meaning to it. Therefore, it is a school therapist's goal to create an environment in which children can engage in meaningful activities to create experiences from which they then learn. Moreover, these activities foster participation, teamwork, generalization and creativity, consequently improving quality of life and wellbeing. Therapists are skilled at altering or grading an activity to match the child's skill level so that he or she can feel a sense of achievement. As Winnie Dunn (1982, p.745) simply stated, "The therapeutic process attempts to provide a situation that contains enough challenge to allow patients an opportunity to adapt to their environment without the stress that increases dysfunction. This is what therapists refer to as the 'just-right' challenge. Locating this fine line is what I consider the art of therapy."

This book is the result of a collaborative effort to develop creative activities that are enjoyable to our students while meeting the *just-right* challenge. It is well documented that occupational therapists collaborate with other professionals to design and adapt activities that lead to accomplishment, mastery, and a sense of purpose and meaning in life (AOTA 2008). If nothing else, therapists are struggling to find ways to become more and more efficient with the always-increasing caseload. Each discipline must deal with increasing demands for personnel, the shortage of qualified teachers, increasing numbers of students, questions concerning healthcare, and how the services of each discipline may fit into the treatment plan for each student (Nord 1973).

The goal is to obtain skill sets that will allow children to be active participants in their day, through fun and challenging activities. This book offers activities that promote development by structuring opportunities for engagement in activities or occupations while facilitating language and skilled motor production. "Occupation" is defined as an activity that occupies someone's attention. Therefore, this book offers a quick reference guide to functional activities that utilize speech, motor, and sensory aspects. The activities are presented with suggested variations that can be used to work with a range of low-level functioning individuals and higher-level individuals functioning with greater independence.

How it works

Therapists' treatment plans focus on evaluating the child and providing interventions to develop, improve, sustain, or restore skills. In the school setting this is achieved by engaging the child in meaningful and purposeful activities. Children engage in play through games, manipulation of toys, interacting with peers, and craft and arts. In order to capture the child's attention and create a positive experience, we use play as the main modality for therapy. These activities can easily be incorporated into a classroom, home, daycare centre, or vocational training program. The use of activity groups facilitates an atmosphere of socialization and peer interaction. An activity group is an effective tool for self-regulation since it offers a realistic yet structured setting which can be graded and modified (Cermak, Stein and Abelson 1973).

Children with autism and other developmental disorders have significant delays in social skills. One study found that participants who engaged in an activity group developed better interpersonal skills than participants who engaged in a verbal group (Mumford 1974). The goal of this book is to find a balance in each activity to address a variety of functional needs. Each activity contains elements of motor skills and language skills combined with a sensory component.

This book is an attempt to empower teachers, therapists, and parents in structuring meaningful activities that children will appreciate. Collaboration in school-based occupational therapy has not been thoroughly studied; research, however, suggests that school-based practitioners are increasingly consulting with teaching staff in the school (Barnes, Schoenfeld and Pierson 1997; Bose and Hinojosa 2008; Case-Smith and Cable 1996). Bazyk *et al.* (2009) found that school therapists who spent twice as much time collaborating with teachers than in direct "pull out" services had students who made significant improvements in their fine motor skills. By applying a non-directive consultation model, therapists use their time educating teachers in how to apply occupational therapy intervention strategies in the classroom.

Speak, Move, Play and Learn with Children on the Autism Spectrum is also about helping children to work toward skills that will lend themselves to gainful employment in the future. Work offers a sense of accomplishment and contribution to one's life that leads to improved self-image (Capo 2001). It also offers opportunities for socialization and community involvement. The skills promoted through these activities allow individuals to gain control over their internal and external environment through functional communication training. The use of assistive technology and sensory integrative techniques helps to promote self-regulation, which is the key to succeeding in employment. Individuals must be able to control their behaviors as well as communicate their wants and needs in the workplace.

Who should do it?

Anyone who engages in occupation and verbal or non-verbal communication can do this! The goal of this book is to provide teachers, therapists, and parents with a quick and easy reference for well-thought-out activities. As school therapists, we get many requests from parents seeking activities to do with their children at home, during long breaks or summer vacation. A major source of stress identified in families with children with autism was the amount of time the individual with autism required, "from the time the child rises until the time they go to sleep" (Degrace 2004, p.545). The activities presented in this book can be implemented during the natural progression of the day in any typical household. For example, these activities can be done during laundry, cooking, cleaning, grooming, and even leisure time. It is our opinion that allowing children to be part of the day's happenings helps them to develop a positive sense of self and a role in the family. We believe that by engaging children in these activities they can develop skills that may be useful in the family's daily living, thus decreasing the amount of time spent in direct care of these children. The activities outlined in this book help individuals develop independence in activities of daily living. They are also practical when seeking employment for an individual with special needs—for example, sorting, stocking, assembling, collating, and cleaning could be useful to a number of employers (Capo 2001).

Watling *et al.* (1999) found that occupational therapists worked more closely with other professionals when working with children with autism than when working with children with other disabilities. In the school setting, children with autism and other disorders have access to an assortment of intervention services, including early intervention, applied behavioral analysis, speech therapy, occupational therapy, adaptive physical education, dietary modification, and so on. Each discipline must deal with the increasing demands for personnel, the shortage of qualified teachers, increasing numbers of students, questions concerning healthcare, and how the services of each discipline may fit into these systems (Nord 1973). Therefore, this book offers a quick reference guide to functional activities that provide speech, motor, and sensory aspects so that therapists can make their day as efficient as possible. These activities also offer a range of methods of implementation to cater for kids across the spectrum, from very low-level functioning to higher-level functioning, so that they always have another level to work up to once they have mastered their current level. The goal is for children to obtain skill sets that will allow them to be active participants in their day through fun and challenging activities.

Where do we do it?

Anywhere people engage in occupation and communication is the perfect place for using this book! It is focused on creative activities that could be used in the school, home, and community settings; however, many therapists working in a variety of settings, including inpatient, outpatient, and acute rehabilitation, also collaborate with other professionals to create treatment plans that maximize their patients' potential. School therapists typically work in the classroom on an inclusive and consultation model. Consultation plays a key role in helping children to succeed throughout the day, not just for the time they are in direct therapy. Literature on inclusion consistently identifies collaboration as the key to its success because students benefit from educational programs that are integrated into the social context of their classrooms (Bose and Hinojosa 2008; Nevin 2000; Sands, Kozleski and French 2000).

Using activity groups is an efficient use of the therapist's time and is beneficial to all students in the class. Utilizing children's daily environment gives them a chance to succeed in the environment in which they spend most of their day. The use of small groups in the classroom allows for maximum opportunities for peer interaction and development of skills in the most realistic and natural environment. A study at Boston University found skill acquisition and transfer was most effective when training occurred in a naturalistic context, rather than a simulated one (Ma, Trombly and Robinson-Podolski 1999). Using small groups in the classroom allows therapists maximal use of their time and resources.

These activities can also be integrated easily into the home or community. The activities in The Store (Chapter 4) are specifically tailored to enhance community involvement while the Activities of Daily Living (Chapter 8) are geared more toward increasing independence in the home and living environment. Being active participants in the community allows individuals to create a bank of personal experiences, which they can learn from and build upon. In a study comparing the effectiveness of personal narratives to that of fictional narratives, children did better with functional aspects of language when personal narratives were used (McCabe *et al.* 2008). For example, children are able to utilize more functional speech when they relate themselves to the activity. Historically, trends in therapy have ranged from introducing a task such as doing laundry through a series of symbols or photographs to mapping and planning the bus systems to get to the laundromat and actually doing laundry. We believe in the idea that actual engagement in activities creates a personal narrative that enables individuals to speak about their experiences and what is meaningful to them.

CHAPTER 1

Social Pragmatic Skills

An individual may say words clearly and use long, complex sentences with correct grammar but still have a communication problem if he or she has not mastered the rules for social language known as *pragmatics.* (American Speech-Language-Hearing Association (ASHA) 2011)

Having the ability to use appropriate greetings and salutations, stay on topic, have good eye contact, and use and understand figurative language is all a part of practicing good social pragmatic skills. Students need to have the ability not only to display but also to interpret subtle changes in facial expression, pitch, tone, body position, and eye contact in order to have complete knowledge of communication. Social pragmatic skills are usually learned during social interactions as a child and are taught to us as manners by our parents. Students on the spectrum have challenges with both displaying and interpreting social language. This makes them appear awkward and different, thereby attracting negative attention such as teasing and bullying. As therapists, educators, and parents, we must be aware of social pragmatic skills and take every opportunity available to practice so that our students can become proficient at communicating beyond words. Here follows a list of social pragmatic skills (adapted from Bowen 2001) to consider during the student's daily activities both at school and at home:

- participating in a conversation by taking turns with a partner(s)

- knowing when to answer and when to ask a question

- noticing and respond to the non-verbal aspects of language; for example, reacting appropriately to the other person's body language and mood while considering their words

- knowing what humor is and when it's OK to be funny

- introducing and maintain a topic appropriately during a conversation

- using segues (smooth transitional phrases) effectively to change a topic

- initiating proper greetings and salutations to fit the situation and place

- joining in with a conversation or interrupting politely

- maintaining appropriate eye contact, body posture, and proximity during a conversation

- maintaining conversational skills appropriate for the place, role, and social situation

- changing the volume of his or her voice for the specific place, such as in a school or playground.

In this book we will be working to improve the child's social pragmatic skills through fun activities and interactions that boost both use and interpretation. Becoming aware of and practicing good social skills will help students become likable and have more friends.

CHAPTER 2

What is Assistive Technology (AT)?

Most people, when asked about assistive technology (AT), think about very complicated, high-tech devices, such as specialized computers, robotic arms, one-of-a kind software, etc. This is only partially true. While some AT devices are fairly complex, there are plenty of lower-level devices available. Do you think we could consider a photograph an AT device? Or a bent spoon? Are these examples of AT? The answer is "they could be." Depending on the context in which they are being used and their purpose, those simple objects can become indispensable in someone's life and can assist in crossing the barrier between "I can't" and "I did it!"

Depending where one looks, different definitions of AT can be found. One of the most widely used definitions is stated in the Technology-Related Assistance for Individuals with Disabilities Act, which defines AT as: "Any item, piece of equipment, or product system, whether acquired commercially off the shelf, modified, or customized, that is used to increase, maintain or improve functional capabilities of individuals with disabilities."

That is a fairly good definition, but it addresses only "equipment." As we all know, any equipment is useless without knowing how to operate it. Here is the second definition from the Act, which describes AT services as: "Any service that directly assists an individual with a disability in the selection, acquisition or use of an assistive technology device."

Therefore, we now have the two major components of AT: we have a device(s) and we have the knowledge of how to use it. The primary focus of this book is on low-level devices that can be acquired "off the shelf" and easily modified by parents and educators to maximize the student's potential for independent functioning.

With whom do we use AT?

As stated in the definition, AT devices are used "to increase, maintain or improve functional capabilities of individuals with disabilities." Unfortunately AT is not a "golden remedy" for every disability and every problem that a child might be experiencing. AT is a tool and a method to increase someone's independence: to allow access to new resources, to fulfill his or her day with purposeful and achievable, goal-oriented activities. Careful evaluation should be conducted prior to implementation of any AT devices.

There are many reasons for a student not being able to perform a certain task. In some cases it is absolutely necessary to introduce AT, but in others it might not be so useful. There are other ways to regain lost skills or to facilitate the development of a new skill. So you have to ask yourself, "Will the person benefit from AT, or will he or she become dependent on it, instead of striving to build a repertoire of required skills?" That question has to be answered prior to the introduction of AT devices. Not doing so might create an undesired dependency on equipment and/or methods that can be difficult to extend across the different settings and environments the person is exposed to.

Where do we use AT?

The simple answer would be "everywhere." Following careful evaluation of a student's needs, and after determining that he or she requires AT, we need to ensure that this student has access to the required devices when and where necessary. For example, if a non-verbal student is being taught to use a communication book during mealtimes at school, he or she has to have access to that book or a replica, with an appropriate assortment of pictures, during a trip to a local restaurant on a weekend. Ensuring unrestricted access to an AT tool or strategy across a variety of settings is the best way to guarantee success in the acquisition of indispensable life skills that will last a lifetime.

When do we use AT?

In general, we would like to use AT in naturally occurring situations and in the context of an activity. Retention of new skills and intrinsic motivation to use AT will be much greater when a student is engaging in a highly enjoyable activity, and when access to such an activity is made possible through the use of the appropriate AT device. For learning to occur, the student needs to be motivated to actively engage in this process.

Does AT work?

In one word: *yes*. It does work. Giving students tools to access previously unreachable areas of their environment is a great accomplishment. It builds self-esteem, enhances environmental access through the refinement of existing skills and aids in the acquisition of new skills. But most importantly, it allows students to increase their independence.

While some devices and techniques require the knowledge and expertise of assistive technology specialists (ATS), there are many situations and everyday items that you can utilize on an everyday basis to enhance the lives of your students. As you are carrying out the activities in this book, carefully evaluate your students' difficulties, discover what it is that they are having trouble doing, and consider why they are having these problems. Find out what it is that they need to complete this task without you doing it for them. Perhaps you might have to change how the task is being performed. Assess whether they need a tool (e.g. a picture, bent spoon, larger keyboard, magnifying glass) to complete this task independently. Just like us, our students have an intrinsic drive and desire to act independently; it's just that some of them need a little bit of help to succeed in their quest.

The great thing about the activities in this book is that the materials needed are all readily available in many environments and the skills can be easily taught. We are striving to give parents, teachers, and caretakers a way of teaching that requires minimal AT knowledge and minimal AT devices for maximum results.

CHAPTER 3

Sensory Integration

This book includes fun, interactive activities that use sensory strategies, not only to pique the interest of the participant, but also to explore sensory effects on behavior. Inefficient interpretation of sensation in the body and environment is associated with impaired behavior, poor academic learning, and delayed motor skills. Delays in communication, behavior, and motor skills are the main reasons why children get referred for support services in the school setting. Occupational therapists working in schools often provide sensory support and strategies in the classroom for the children on their caseload. Sensory integrative-based therapy utilizes meaningful therapeutic activities that include enhanced sensation to facilitate active participation and adaptive reactions. Sensory integration theory will be briefly discussed here; however, the theory and practice framework is well researched and documented.

In 1979, Jean Ayres defined sensory integration as "A neurological process that organizes sensation from one's own body and the environment and makes it possible to use the body effectively within the environment" (p.11). According to sensory integration theory, learning is dependent on the ability to take in, process, and integrate sensation and use that information to plan and organize behavior and movement patterns for performing every day activities (Ayres 1972). Our goal as therapists is to create the optimal learning environment so that the child can access educational, occupational, and/or vocational opportunities. This includes: altering or adapting the activity to fit the child's skill level; modifying the environment, including set-up of materials and decreasing clutter or visual distractions; and altering a child's arousal level to fit the environment in which he or she will be interacting. A focused, calm, and quiet state of arousal is associated with the optimal learning level.

Introducing sensory input, specifically in the tactile, proprioceptive, and vestibular systems, is a way of achieving altered states of arousal. For example, heavy proprioceptive input through deep pressure touch like a massage is calming, while light touch is alerting to the nervous system, and both can elicit very different arousal levels. There are other sensory systems (visual, olfactory, gustatory, and auditory); however, we will focus on the tactile, proprioceptive, and vestibular systems, as they are key elements in the sensory integration theory.

Deficits in tactile processing occur when inefficient processing of a touch sensation is perceived through our skin. Children with over-responsive tactile systems, or children who are tactile defensive, may respond negatively to an unexpected or light touch. These children typically avoid contact and do not engage with age-appropriate activity materials, such as paint, glue, feathers, or shaving cream. These children are often resistant to bath time or are picky eaters. A child with an under-responsive tactile system may constantly touch objects and people or have decreased reaction to injuries. These children have difficulty manipulating utensils, crayons, and scissors. They might require extra tactile stimulation to learn about object properties.

The proprioceptive system allows us to know where our body is in space. Children with deficits in this system have poor awareness of their body and positioning. They appear uncoordinated or clumsy, and often have a difficult time maintaining a calm and focused body. Children with inefficient processing in the proprioceptive system often seek out heavy input by crashing or bumping into objects. Poor proprioceptive processing is often associated with difficulty with handwriting skills.

The vestibular system is located in our inner ear and it tells us where our head and body are in relation to gravity. This system is important for overall muscle tone, balance, and coordination. Children who exhibit over-responsiveness to vestibular input show intolerance to movement or are cautious with gross motor play on playgrounds. Children with an under-responsiveness to vestibular input may show little response to movement. These children usually spin more than other children and do not appear to get dizzy. They demonstrate an increased tolerance to movement, tend to move excessively, and cannot remain still. These children are often bouncing on furniture, rocking, or assuming an upside-down position. These children commonly have poor postural control and appear to be slumped over or to lean constantly on objects. The activities that follow highlight ways to integrate these key sensory components into fun, entertaining activities that facilitate speech and language. These activities can be adapted in many ways to fit older and younger children as well as cognitively impaired children.

CHAPTER 4

The Store

What is it?

"The Store," simply put, is a place for students to go not only to "buy" items but also to learn a multi-modality means of communication. This means that when a student participates in this activity they are exposed to picture exchange and signs or gestures, and are encouraged to use vocalizations. The Store uses highly desired items and activities to motivate students to learn communication as well as social pragmatic skills.

Picture exchange was designed for non-verbal students with autism, and has been used successfully to support communication. When using picture exchange, a student will touch or hand a picture of the desired item to the communication partner (who can be an adult or peer who will follow through with the routine). In return, the student receives the desired item. The desired item can be food, a toy, or an activity, such as a walk. Students will gradually add more pictures for their choices, will eventually keep them in a binder, wallet, or on a choice board, and will move across distance to obtain their items. When The Store routine has been practiced and mastered, the students may then become the "Storekeeper," running and cleaning The Store and stocking the shelves. Anyone in school or at home can set up a "Store."

Why it works

Using highly motivating items will encourage students to focus their attention and do their best to obtain the items. When the item is given to the students directly after the exchange, they begin to associate the picture, sign, and/or verbalization with getting the things they want.

Once that association has been made, the routine can be modified to add more steps and eventually have the students leaving their seats, walking to another room, making an exchange with their best communicative effort, and walking back to their seat. In a nutshell, it is the motivation of obtaining the desired item that establishes the communication routine. Once the routine is set, new variables and skills can be introduced, such as new items, pragmatics, distance, and even money.

This chapter will direct you through a series of activities designed to establish multi-modality communication. It is recommended that the student begin with picture exchange communication as it has proven to be the easiest for the students who have successfully completed The Store activities. Sign or gesture and verbalizations can come after the routine has been mastered. Of course, all students are different and some may find it less challenging to begin with sign and gesture. Finally, be aware of each student's limitations and make the task (picture exchange, sign, or vocalization) well within their abilities to avoid frustration and ensure successful completion of all Store activities.

The Store activities are highly effective in the classroom, in one-to-one sessions, and in groups both large and small. Items sold at The Store should initially be highly desirable. If the item is a food item, it should be a small piece so that it is consumed quickly and the student is ready for another turn. For example, if a student wants an apple, cut the apple into ten slices so that he or she has ten opportunities to request "apple."

Multiple copies of each picture or picture icon should be made, and they should be protected with lamination or contact paper for each student to use in The Store activities as part of their personal communication systems.

Success strategies and best practices for The Store

- To promote flexibility and generalization, the station used in The Store activity should be portable so that this activity can be moved around the school or home environment. A bin with many baggies filled with the various items works well.

- Use and encourage picture exchange with choice boards, wallets, binders and voice output in conjunction with voicing and sign language. The more communication formats the students are familiar with, the better they will be at expressing their wants and needs across environments.

- Use as much prompting as necessary to establish the routine of The Store, then fade prompts to the natural environment.

- When first introducing The Store activity to the students, use highly motivating reinforcers to ensure high interest. Gradually fade unhealthy and inappropriate reinforcers for a variety of healthier and more suitable rewards. To guarantee success, introduce The Store around snack time and offer favorite snacks.

- Keep all items in The Store out of reach, but within sight of the students.

- If a student comes to The Store and is disruptive or has inappropriate behavior, simply direct that student back to his or her seat where he or she can be prompted to make better choices and watch the examples of the other students.

- Make mistakes. Occasionally, hand the students the wrong items, an empty bag, or do not notice their presence at The Store. This lets them problem solve, ask for help, or figure out how to get your attention.

- After students indicate their choice via picture exchange, encourage them to verbalize and sign the name of the item they are requesting.

- Between The Store 4 and The Store 5, begin to add social skills and manners. "Hello," "please," "thank you," and "goodbye" should all be mastered and expected at every turn.

- Snacks should be given out in small pieces to allow for many trials and should not be eaten until the student returns to his or her seat.

- New students will catch up. No need to begin at The Store 1.

- After The Store routine is established, reduce prompting and calling students' names by using the phrases, "Who's next?" or "When Cindy is done, it's your turn."

- Take the students on a field trip to a real store after they have mastered making decisions and purchases.

Making Pictures for Your Communication System

Purpose: To create a set of pictures to use for The Store activity, and for daily communication with family, friends, teachers, and caregivers. Allowing students to choose and assemble their picture exchange system will increase their success in using pictures to communicate.

Materials: Creating a personalized set of pictures for a group or individual is easy with the help of an internet image search (we use Google image search). If the internet is not available then use wrappers, box tops, magazines, newspapers, or photographs. Contact paper or lamination will protect your pictures and Velcro will make them easy to display.

Description: If you are using an internet image search, simply type the name of the item/activity into the search bar and have the students choose the image they want, then copy and paste the image(s) into a blank document. Print the images, cover with lamination or contact paper, and, if desired, add Velcro.

Have the students type the name of the item/activity and operate the computer. It may take longer, but the learning opportunity is well worth the extra time. Students can also help with covering and Velcro.

Using magazines, wrappers, and newspapers is a good way to get students involved in making their picture exchange systems. Students can look through the pages to find the pictures they want, cut them out, and cover the pictures. Students can also look around their environment to find wrappers, labels, or other packaging to represent the desired items. For example, the small sticker on an apple from the grocery store can represent an apple, or the label from the bubble container can be used to represent blowing bubbles.

Give the students as much freedom as possible to choose, cut out, and cover their picture representations. It's not always pretty, but it provides a sense of ownership.

A combination of both computer-generated and homemade images or representations works very well and lets all students participate at their level in designing a communication system.

34

Variations:

- Turn this activity into a scavenger hunt by providing students with a list of items/activities and letting them find representations.

- Students can duplicate their picture exchange system to use with wallets, binders, choice boards, and personal picture exchange systems.

The Store 1—Establishing the Communication Exchange

Purpose: The Store 1 establishes the communication exchange, turn taking, sequencing, visual perception skills, reading, activities of daily living, and motor control. This activity can be completed in a small group, classroom or one-to-one session.

Materials: The instructor should have one or two highly preferred items for each student with a picture or picture icon to match the item. Each picture should have the written word included. Make multiple copies of the pictures and be sure to protect them by laminating them or using contact paper. Each picture will be used throughout The Store activities and become part of the student's personal picture exchange communication system.

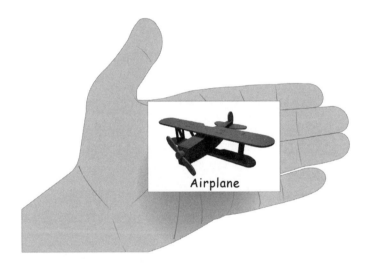

Description: The instructor announces:

"It's Store time."

All students are instructed to take their seats and wait their turn. The instructor then approaches them, greets them with a handshake, high five, or wave, and welcomes them to The Store. The student who follows directions most readily and sits most quietly gets the first turn. The instructor chooses the student who is ready first by saying, "Today I will start with Arlene because she is sitting quietly and waiting for her turn." The instructor then places a picture of Arlene's favorite item on her desk and asks, "What would you like?" If there is no response, she is prompted to touch the picture or hand it to the instructor. The student is immediately given the item, as well as verbal praise, when she touches or passes the picture.

So that each student can anticipate his or her turn, the instructor moves in an orderly, predictable pattern around the room, following the same procedure as above and providing each student with a favorite item. If a student is not in his or her seat, the instructor prompts, "Where is Bret? It is Bret's turn." If Bret does not return to his seat in a reasonable amount of time, the next student gets his or her turn and Bret is again prompted to take his seat and wait for his next turn.

The Store 1 activity should take approximately 20–30 minutes but can last twice as long as that if the children are willing to pay attention. Each student should be given several turns at The Store.

Variations:

- Use a student helper to be the Storekeeper by either providing the picture or handing students their favorite items.

- Duplicate this activity by incorporating different variations into the daily schedule; for example, by offering a favorite snack or drink during snack time, or a leisure activity during a break.

- When a student has difficulty touching or passing the picture, a third person can help guide the student with hand-over-hand prompting until he or she can follow the routine independently.

The Store 2—Adding Distance

Purpose: Once a student has mastered the single picture exchange from their seat, distance is added. Students learn turn taking, communication, sequencing, and attention skills. This is a good step to begin greetings and salutations.

Materials: The instructor should have several highly preferred items for each student with a corresponding picture representation. Pictures should be labeled with the word they are representing. Pictures from The Store 1 activity may be reused for this activity. This activity will initially take two instructors.

Description: The instructor begins by setting up a station for The Store. Round tables, kitchen tables, or desks make great stations. Items should be within sight, but out of reach. A choice board is posted within reach and sight of the students who come to The Store. The instructor now proclaims,

"It's Store time! Please take your seats and wait your turn."

The student who is ready first, sitting in his or her seat and looking at the instructor, gets the first trip to The Store. The instructor who is the "Storekeeper" can anticipate what the student will want and place that picture alone on the choice board.

Students are encouraged to walk or are escorted to the station; they then make their choice of desired item by taking the picture from the choice board and handing it to the Storekeeper. The Storekeeper then immediately hands the student the desired item and the student is directed or escorted back to his or her seat.

Moving clockwise in a predictable sequence, each student gets a turn to go to The Store. Students who are not seated or do not come back to their seat when prompted get the opportunity to watch their classmates obtain desired items and model the routine. But they are not given reinforcers until it is their turn again.

After a few rounds, the Storekeeper can begin encouraging verbalizations, sign/gesture, and social pragmatic skills by greeting the students, modeling the request, and obtaining a thank you with a farewell after making an exchange. Students are greeted in front of The Store prior to making their choice. The Storekeeper then asks the student,

"What would you like today?" and displays the choice board with a predetermined desired item. After the student indicates the choice by picture exchange, verbalizations, and/or sign, the Storekeeper hands the student the item, but does not let go until the student indicates thank you, eye contact, and farewell. The student then goes back to their seat to enjoy the purchase.

Variations:

- The station can be a portable cart or kiosk that can be easily moved from location to location.

- The station can be set up in another room or closet so that students are encouraged to generalize skills.

- Choice boards can be replaced with wallets, binders, and/or voice output devices.

- Students can take turns being the Storekeeper.

- Desired items can be distributed in reusable bags or jars with lids to encourage fine motor skills.

The Store 3—Visual Discrimination

Purpose: This lesson introduces visual discrimination to The Store activity. In addition to learning the valuable skills of visual scanning and discriminating, the student will reinforce the prowess of turn taking, listening, sequencing, opening containers, and social skills.

Materials: You will need one or two highly preferred items and corresponding pictures for each student. Items and pictures may be carried over from The Store 2. You will also need one distractor picture with the corresponding object on hand. I usually use a 2 inch by 2 inch (5 cm by 5 cm) square of colored paper, but you can use anything that is neutral to the student (sock, rock, paper plate, bag, etc). Place pictures of the distractor and desired item on the choice board, approximately 2–3 inches (5–7 cm) apart.

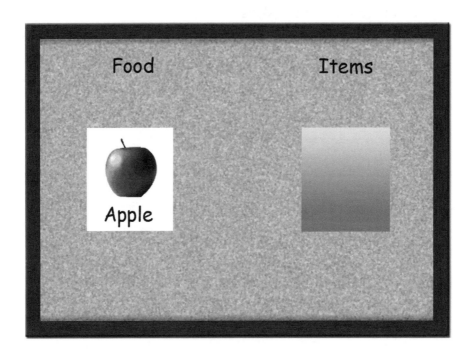

Description: The instructor begins by setting up the station for The Store. The same station as The Store 2 can be used. All items should be within sight, but out of reach of the students. The Instructor announces,

"It's Store time! Please take your seats and wait your turn to go to The Store."

The student who is the first to be sitting in their seat looking at the instructor gets to have the first trip to The Store. The Storekeeper places a picture of the desired item and a distractor on the choice board. As the student reaches the station, the instructor encourages a greeting and asks, "What would you like from The Store?" The student will then have the opportunity to choose from the two pictures. The Storekeeper immediately gives the student the item indicated by the picture.

Be prepared: Students who have not developed visual discrimination skills and choose the distractor may become frustrated. *Do not* exchange the distractor for the desired item. Simply redirect the student to his or her seat and verbally reinforce making good choices and waiting for his or her next turn to obtain the desired item. Make sure that every student who has chosen a distractor gets another chance to make the "right" choice and is given the support needed to make the correct choice. Support can be hand-over-hand, partial physical prompt, and a verbal or indirect prompt. The Store activity should end when every student has made a correct choice of their desired item.

After the student receives the requested item, encourage a salutation and have the student return to their seat. Moving in a predictable, clockwise sequence, each student can have three or four turns to shop at The Store.

Variations:

- Move The Store station to different locations around the room or outside the door to encourage flexibility.

- Desired items can be placed in reusable baggies or twist-top bottles for fine motor coordination.

The Store 4—Making Purposeful, Deliberate Choices

Purpose: To reinforce and build upon the skills of visual discrimination, scanning, turn taking, sequencing, listening, following directions, and fine motor.

Materials: You will need one to three highly preferred items and the corresponding picture with a written word. You will also need one or two distractor pictures, a choice board, binder, wallet, and/or voice output device. All choices from all the students are placed on the choice board in two categories (usually "food" and "items") along with the distractor(s).

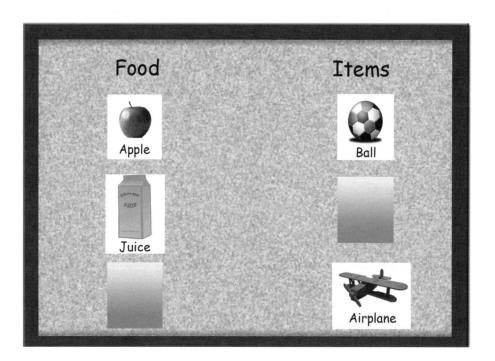

Description: The Store remains the same as in the previous activities. The choice board is displayed in front of The Store with all available items visible. The instructor declares,

"It's Store time!"

However, by now most students will anticipate Store time due to the station and choice board set-up, and quietly take their seats. The student who is sitting and looking at the instructor without being prompted will be the first to go to The Store. The instructor should verbally praise the student for paying attention.

As the student reaches The Store, the Storekeeper should prompt a greeting by shaking the student's hand and offering a verbal greeting. After the student greets the Storekeeper, he or she can make a choice by taking a picture of the desired item and handing it to the Storekeeper. The Storekeeper places the item into the student's hand, but does not let go until the student indicates thank you and makes eye contact. The Storekeeper gives a farewell and the student is sent back to his or her seat.

Be prepared: Give students exactly what they have indicated on the picture. Do not attempt to anticipate what they want at this point and do not prompt student choices. It is important that students discriminate between items independently. They will only choose a non-preferred item once or twice. Moving in a predictable clockwise sequence, everyone should have three to five turns, or more.

Variations:

- Send two students to The Store at the same time to practice waiting in line.

- Move The Store to different locations and open it at various times of the day to support flexibility and generalization.

- Introduce several new items by showing the students the items and corresponding pictures prior to beginning the activity.

- Prior to The Store activity, have several students be Assistant Storekeepers by filling reusable bags and containers with Store items.

The Store 5—Building Sentence Length and Complexity

Purpose: To reinforce skills acquired thus far in The Store while increasing proficiency in expressive language.

Materials: Continue using highly preferred items with corresponding pictures with the written word on them. Begin adding variety into The Store via color and/or size. For example, have a red and green apple available or have several colors and sizes of soft ball to choose from. Add color picture representations on the choice board (usually along the bottom) with the corresponding written word. To indicate sizes simply use written words such as "big" and "small." Last, provide two to three sentence strips with the sentence starter, "I want——."

Description: Prepare The Store by adding additional color and size items so that the students can see but not reach them. The instructor proclaims,

"It's Store time! Let's get ready for The Store."

Any new items and their corresponding pictures are presented to each student and they are encouraged to touch or taste them. The student who is listening and following directions best gets the first trip to The Store.

When an item is chosen by the student, he or she is directed to place the item on the sentence strip and hand the entire sentence strip to the Storekeeper. The Storekeeper reads the sentence strip with the student and then retrieves the item. If there is more than one choice due to size or color, the Storekeeper prompts the student to add that descriptor to the sentence strip.

Encourage social interactions and do not let go of the desired item until the student indicates, "Thank you." Continue in a predictable pattern around the room until all students have had several turns to go shopping at The Store. At this level of The Store it usually takes one to two months for students to become proficient at using sentence strips and descriptors.

Variations:

- The Storekeeper should occasionally make mistakes such as handing the student the wrong item or an empty bag to encourage problem solving and asking for help.

- To encourage student acceptance of new items, the Storekeeper can give some away free with the "purchase" of desired items. The pairing of new items to desired items will expand the students' tolerance for novel experiences and flavors.

- Continue building choice boards, wallets, binders, and voice output devices, and categorizing the choices into food, drinks, leisure activities, music, etc.

- Have all forms of communication available for students to make choices. This builds flexibility and generalization skills.

The Store 6—Using Money

Purpose: To reinforce and build upon skills acquired in The Store activities, adding purchasing. Students will learn to exchange coins and dollars for items at The Store.

Materials: Use all the same items, pictures, and forms of communication as for previous Store activities, with the addition of coins and dollar bills. Put coins into a zipped coin purse and a dollar into a wallet.

Description: Instruction begins by showing all the students a dollar, having them pull it out of the wallet, and opening the coin purse to see a penny, nickel, dime, and quarter inside. Don't worry if the students do not have a concept of money at this point; they will understand it soon. Place the wallet and coin purse within the students' reach—in front of the choice board works well.

Follow all the same procedures as in The Store 5 by building a sentence strip and handing it to the Storekeeper. The Storekeeper then reads the sentence strip with the student and requests payment. For example, "You want a red apple? That will cost a dollar." Use a secondary prompter to help the student retrieve a dollar from the wallet and hand it to the Storekeeper. The Storekeeper immediately gives the student the item, remembering not to let go until the student indicates thank you, and sends him or her back to his or her seat.

Every student at every ability level will have the ability to find the dollar in the wallet and "pay" for their item within two to three trials. After mastering the dollar exchange, try a quarter, then a dime, and so on.

Variations:

- Have the price of every item displayed on the item for extra visual support.

- Money can be placed in the students' pockets or backpacks to duplicate a functional situation.

- Adjust payment to the individual student goals. If a student has the goal of identifying coins, then focus on single coins. Another student may have the goal of counting coins, in which case focus on coin combinations.

- Add a cash register and cashier to this activity to teach vocational skills and maximize generalization.

- Use the dollar-up strategy to teach the important life skill of purchasing. Give the cashier the number of full dollars the item costs plus one more to account for the change. For example, if an item costs $2.59, give the cashier two dollars plus one more for a total of three dollars and then wait for change.

- Begin having students wait in line, leaving a comfortable space between themselves and the person ahead of them. Start with two students in line and gradually increase the challenge by adding more students.

The Store 7—Adding Comments and Vocational Skills

Purpose: To use the highly motivating activity of The Store to encourage comments and yes/no responses, and to support vocational goals by encouraging participation in The Store upkeep and management.

Materials: At this point The Store should be full of items organized into categories, descriptors, sentence strips, money, wallet, coin purse, and several formats for choices, including the choice board, binder, voice output device, and wallet. The last component to add to The Store is the visual support for the students to make comments. Pictures of the words "Yes" and "No" can be placed on the choice board so that students can answer questions regarding purchases. Additional conversation supports can be added, such as emotion pictures, school pictures, weather pictures, and numbers. Instructors can add additional picture supports according to different student goals.

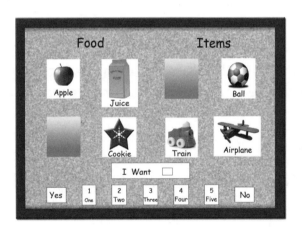

Description: Students should be encouraged to organize The Store and prepare items for display in The Store. For example, they can cut up a variety of apples, place a few grapes in a bag, fill a water pitcher, restock

SPEAK, MOVE, PLAY AND LEARN WITH CHILDREN ON THE AUTISM SPECTRUM

napkins, and make sure leisure items are in workable order. After The Store is prepared and restocked, the instructor announces,

"It's Store time!"

And a student is chosen to be first in line.

After the student greets the Storekeeper, the Storekeeper will ask the student a question such as, "How are you?" or "What is the weather like?" Then the Storekeeper will supply the visual supports for the student to answer that question. Once the question is answered, the student is invited to choose an item, construct a sentence strip, pay, indicate thank you, and return to his or her seat.

Upon returning to their seats, students should prompt the next participant in The Store by indicating, "It's your turn." After all students have had several turns, they can clean, restock, and prepare for the next time they get to go to The Store. The instructor should prompt conversation such as, "What did you buy?" or "Did you like the new items?"

Variations:

- Add a cash register and cashier to your Store.

- Choose a student to help out as an Assistant Storekeeper. Give that student an apron, badge, or hat to indicate Assistant Storekeeper status.

- Move The Store to various rooms or locations and make the announcement, "The Store is in the cafeteria today," to support flexibility and generalization.

- Students can practice patience by waiting in line for their turn. Teach appropriate distance and waiting etiquette.

CHAPTER 5

Simply Sensory

It is important to remember that the main occupation in childhood is play. The activities included in this chapter are geared to maximizing the child's interest by utilizing fun and exciting materials. Providing this motivating element encourages children to engage and participate in structured activities that allow opportunities for success.

You will find a range of novel items used in this chapter, such as shaving cream, noodles, dirt, various scents, and many others. If children appear hesitant to touch certain substances or materials, encourage them to smell the substances or describe how they look while continuing to encourage them to feel the substance. If they display a strong behavioral reaction, provide them with a utensil, such as a paintbrush, or protective clothing, such as gloves, to minimize their hesitation. Tactile reactions are typically strongest for those children who are defensive; therefore, it is crucial to engage them in a playful environment while allowing and respecting their choice to say "no." This will help build their trust in you so next time you challenge them they are more willing to engage.

The olfactory sense has a strong link to our emotional state and there are various scents that elicit different reactions. Some scents are calming. Calming scents can be used in times of behavioral breakdowns when the child is not responding to verbal instruction. Allowing the child to take a few deep breaths of a calming scent pillow may help pacify him or her enough to transition to a safer or quieter area. If you have children who are difficult to engage, switching between different scents may help. Explore various strategies to find one that works best for that particular student. However, a word to the wise: after working with these children for many years, we have come to learn that they are not always consistent in their wants and needs.

It is important to encourage the children to complete as much of the activity as possible independently, providing just enough support for them to be successful in the task. For example, if a child struggles with scissors, provide self-opening scissors or an alternative adaptive scissor, instead of cutting for the child. Know your children and their capabilities. If they are too young or cognitively impaired to manipulate common classroom tools, focus on the assembly or steps of the activity.

When setting up the activity, strategically place materials and tools so that children will have to share and/or initiate conversations with each other. It is important to encourage them to look one another in the face and use names if possible. Encourage the children to maintain appropriate "personal space" within the group setting, and model asking a peer to share materials. Provide a visual demonstration of the expectations in the group setting, and explain how they should manage their body, eyes, and ears during the activities. In this chapter, emphasis is placed on the social interactions and communication between the students, and their ability to engage in a natural conversation. Encourage the children to comment on each other's work and ask questions about each other. Attempt to minimize visual distractions and clutter in their workspace. Pick a child who is exhibiting appropriate behavior to pass out materials or gather others' work.

Some behavioral and social difficulties may be a manifestation of an underlying sensory processing issue. It is therefore important to teach our children how to recognize their own body's needs, and also how to manage them in a socially appropriate way. For example, it would not be appropriate for a 25-year-old to carry a chewy toy all day to fulfil his oral motor needs; however, we can incorporate crunchy, hard foods into his daily routine. The same concept applies to providing children with tactile, vestibular, and proprioceptive input periodically throughout the day to help maintain an optimal level of arousal.

Try to take note of a child's behavioral responses and energy levels during and following a largely gross motor activity. Does she spend her time engaging in unstructured play, such as hand flapping, spinning, or twirling, during a structured activity? Does she exhibit behavior that could be characterized as "seeking movement?" Is it difficult for the child to transition? Is she able to maintain safe hands and body with her peers? Does she seem more calm or focused after recess or sports? Observing these types of behavioral trends will help you to learn how to encourage the child to engage in various activities that will help with self-regulation.

Oral Motor Fun

Purpose: This activity will help students to organize oral motor sensation and coordination, and to strengthen blowing, chewing, sucking, and diadochinetic skills. Oral Motor Fun also supports labeling, verb+ing, fine motor, and group pragmatics. This activity works well individually and with groups.

Materials: You will need an assortment of blowing and sucking tools such as; horns, whistles, bubbles, balloons, straws, toy or real wind instruments, a cup and a large ziplock bag per student and instructor. Suckers, frozen juice pops, lollipops, gummies and/or licorice are great oral motor stimulators as well as motivators. Unbreakable mirrors provide excellent visual feedback and are a good addition to this activity if available.

Description: Prepare a zipper lock sandwich bag for each student with two or three blow toys, straws, suckers, and/or balloons. Have each student write their name on a bag. Have the students place mirrors in front of themselves before choosing a cup and filling it with water to about half full. Students should be sitting at a table so that they can see each other and themselves in the mirrors.

The instructor announces, "It's time for Oral Motor Fun." Students open and remove the items from their bags. The instructor picks up a whistle, demonstrates blowing, and encourages all students to follow along and blow their whistles. When students have practiced for a few minutes, the instructor says, "Five more blows and then in the bag. Ready, Blow 1, Blow 2, Blow 3, Blow 4, Blow 5, and now put all the whistles into the bag."

Provide the same routine for all items in the bag; allow a few minutes to practice structured blowing or sucking and then put the item back into the bag. Any edible items or liquids via a straw should be the last activities in Oral Motor Fun. Every week add one more item to the bag for more practice and a fun surprise.

When this activity is complete all the items will be put back into the bags. Students can zip close the bags and return both the bag and cup to a specified drawer or box.

 Be aware of your students' limitations. If a student bites plastic, then use cardboard and always keep a hand on the toy or food item. If choking is a challenge, then do not give gummies or large pieces of chewy food.

Variations:

- Add music and have the students blow horns or whistles to the music.

- For more of a challenge when sucking, use apple sauce, milkshakes, or pudding.

- Students can blow ping pong balls, cotton balls, feathers, balloons, or paper balls across the floor or table with or without straws. They can have races or play a soccer-type game while blowing the balls and having fun.

Scent Sense

Purpose: This activity promotes sensory awareness, fine motor skills, grasping practice, describing attributes, comparing and contrasting. See the Appendix for list of descriptors.

Materials: You will need between three and six empty plastic bottles that are long and squeezable. Old plastic ketchup bottles and generic picnic condiment bottles work best.

Ingredients: Cotton balls or tissue paper, scented oils, fragrant fruit peels, extracts, peanut butter, jellies, perfumes, or room air fresheners.

Description: First you should choose a student to volunteer to make a scented item. He should get either a cotton ball or a piece of tissue paper. Then have the child describe how the cotton ball feels. Let the child pick a scent from those that you have available and saturate the cotton ball or tissue with the scent. Afterwards, have the child place the cotton ball or tissue in the bottle and close it. Repeat this step a few more times with different children picking different scents until you have enough bottles to start the comparison.

Get one of the bottles and squeeze the scented air from the bottle into their noses. Make sure you get everyone. Next, ask what the children smell and put their responses on the board or on a piece of butcher paper.

After you have gathered all the responses from the children, begin to compare and contrast the scents. For example, "I can see that you guys thought the orange peels and bananas smelled sweet; that means they are similar. Can someone tell me which scent was their favorite? Which did you like the least?" The children will get a chance to explore their sense of smell and describe attributes while comparing elements on this fun activity.

Variations:

- Give the kids an opportunity to bring different items that are very strong smelling from home. Then have them share their personal scent with the other children.

- Plug-in room scent inserts are also a great substitution to use.

- To add a little challenge, see if the kids can tell the difference between lime, lemon, and orange peel scents.

- Other scents that you can use are dollops of scented lotions, pungent spices, pieces of scented candles, and soap (cut into a piece that will fit inside the bottle).

Be careful to not put any liquids or dust-type particles that can be squeezed out of the bottle and irritate the nose or eyes.

Remember to make sure that 90 percent of the bottle is air and only about 10 percent of it is filled with the scented item. This ensures that you are squirting air into the noses and nothing else.

Stretch for Comfort

Purpose: This activity develops fine motor skills and provides students with increased tactile input. It improves strength, endurance, balance, and overall gross motor control, including motor planning, and promotes bilateral integration and crossing midline. Assuming yoga positions provides increased vestibular and proprioceptive input.

Materials: You will need pinwheel pasta (for the head), linguine (for the back), spaghetti (for arms and legs), and elbow pasta (for shoulders and hips). You will also need construction paper, glue, and printouts of yoga positions.

Description: Place the different types of noodles in a large bowl and gently stir to mix up the noodles. Allow the children to submerge their hand and explore the noodles; this provides increased tactile input. Make sure to include descriptions for anything they feel. Are the noodles hard? Crunchy? Slippery?

After playing with the noodles for a while, have children trace or copy (depending on their skill level) the yoga poses with the dried noodles using each type of noodles for their specified body parts as outlined in the materials section. Make sure to glue the noodles to the paper, all the while labeling the different body parts as the student glues them on. Have the child glue three or four poses on different pieces of paper.

Once the glue dries, arrange the poses into a booklet form. Have the child write or trace the name of the poses on each page. You now have a book of Yoga poses. Play soothing music and have the child move through the poses on each page making sure they say the name of the pose they want to do next. Yoga helps enhance self-awareness in kids. Encourage them to breathe deep belly breaths while thinking of pleasant thoughts.

Progression of poses:

Variations:

- For increased proprioceptive input, add weights to the child's ankles and wrists.

- For more advanced students, have the student label the body parts with scientific names such as scapula, femur, cranium, etc.

- You can do this book over a week or month, adding a new pose each time you see them. By the end they should have a rather large collection that they can take home and share with their parents.

 Remember to breathe, breathe, and breathe!

57

Spring Seed

Purpose: This fun activity allows children to explore different textures and tactile sensations. It helps facilitate a range of grasping patterns for improved fine motor development. It utilizes multi-stepped directions and sequencing during the construction of a booklet. This activity facilitates language development through sequential storytelling.

Materials: For this activity you will need construction paper (4 inches by 6 inches; 10 cm by 15 cm), scissors, cotton balls, glue, and paintbrushes. You will also need shelled sunflower seeds, blades of grass, blue-colored water, dirt, and flower or clover stems.

Description: Have the children sit at a group table and encourage them to use friendly requests when sharing materials. Continue to recognize and praise positive behavior and good listening skills. Have the children cut approximately six 4-by-6 inch squares out of the white construction paper per booklet. Provide a demonstration for each step with a verbal instruction so that they have a model to work from.

In the middle of the first page have the children glue a shelled sunflower seed. Discuss what a seed is and where it comes from. Encourage the children to taste a sunflower seed and discuss the salty flavor.

For the second page, draw a yellow sun in the upper half of the page. Spread glue with a paintbrush on the lower third of a piece of construction paper. Put a generous amount of potting soil in a bowl and have the children sprinkle soil with their fingers or a spoon onto the paper so that glue is covered. Shake off excess potting soil into the bowl of soil. Glue a few sunflower seeds randomly dispersed within the soil. Discuss why seeds need sunlight and soil to grow.

Repeat the pattern of the second page for the third page; however, this time add frayed cotton balls for clouds instead of the sun in the sky. Provide a small dish with blue colored water and have the children dip their fingers into the water and drip "rain" on the page. Continue to discuss how seeds need water to grow. Discuss during which season flowers grow and why.

On the fourth page, the children repeat the process of the second page but add grass blades and clover stems growing out of the soil.

For the last page, repeat the previous page but add wild flower petals at the end of the clover stems to depict a sunflower, or draw yellow sunflowers around the clover stems. Glue an unshelled sunflower seed in the middle of the flower. Discuss how the flower makes seeds, relating it back to the first page. Once the glue has dried, have the child create a cover page for the book.

Have the child practice narrating the story of how a seed becomes a flower. It can be as simple as, "Here is a seed, the seed needs sun and dirt and water to grow, the seed grows out of the dirt and makes a flower, which makes more seeds," or more complex details including root structures, photosynthesis, or precipitation. Encourage students to share their story with their peers, and family members.

Variations:

- Have the children go on a scavenger hunt to find the outdoor items such as dirt, grass blades, clover stems, and wild flowers. Provide them with either a visual list with pictures depicting the items or a written list, depending on each child's cognitive level. Have them scoop the dirt with both hands, pull on the grass blades, and pick the wild flowers, facilitating various grasping patterns.

- If children are resistant to submerging their hands in various textures, use utensils such as spoons to scoop or pipettes to drip water.

If possible, have children shell the sunflower seeds themselves for increased fine motor practice. Cut the very tips of the shell for easier access to the seed.

What's in the Bag?

Purpose: To promote sensory integration and increase use of descriptors, categorization, in-hand manipulation, predicting, guessing, and creativity. This game is a favorite and the children never, ever get tired of it. See the Appendix for descriptor suggestions.

Materials: You will need one cloth bag and a variety of foods or objects with textures, smells, sounds, and flavors (popcorn, lemons, strawberries, feathers, classroom or household items, the secret ingredient for a cooking or artistry group…).

Description: This guessing game can be played prior to groups with the "secret ingredient or item" in the bag or as a complete group exercise. The teacher puts an item into a cloth bag out of sight of the students. The teacher begins by showing the bag to the students so they can look and guess size and weight. The teacher then shakes the bag in front of the group and next to each student's ear asking, "What do you hear?" He or she repeats what each student hears and moves on to touch. Students then take a turn putting their hand into the bag to feel only the secret object. Students should describe what they feel and may at that time make a guess. The teacher repeats what each student has felt so that others can hear it again. Finally, the object is revealed and the teacher reviews the attributes. Each student will get their own piece of the original to touch, squish, smell and experience.

If the item in the bag has a smell, like an orange or cinnamon stick, have the students smell their finger tips for clues.

Variations:

- Put more than one object into the bag and have the students compare and contrast the objects.

- Cut out letters of the alphabet and numbers to put into the bag.

- Students should ask each other, "What's in the bag," and "How does it feel and smell?"

SPEAK, MOVE, PLAY AND LEARN WITH CHILDREN ON THE AUTISM SPECTRUM

Whatcha Got?

Purpose: This activity targets a skill called stereognosis, which is the ability to identify an object through touch alone. It helps improve tactile discrimination and tactile processing. This activity promotes the use of descriptive language to learn adjectives such as smooth, soft, small, etc. This activity provides the opportunity to discuss characteristics and properties for building the concept of similarity and difference. See the Appendix for a list of descriptors.

Materials: You will need pairs of items similar in size and shape. For example: 2 sticks, 2 marbles, 2 feathers, 2 rocks, 2 small pine cones, 2 small shells, 2 cotton balls, 2 dice. Use common items found around the child's environment. Place the pairs of items into a drawstring or paper bag.

Description: Reach your hand into the bag and pull out one item. Have the child describe the item using adjectives and descriptors. For example, "This is a marble; it is small, smooth, and round." Allow the child to explore the item with his or hands. Ask the child to place one hand into the bag and find the same item. Encourage the child to use his or her hands and not eyes.

Variations:

- To increase the challenge you can divide each item into two bags and ask the child to put each hand in one bag. Have the child pull out matching items.

- To increase the challenge you can place foam or plastic letters or numbers into the bag and ask the child to pull out specific letters or numbers.

- This activity can be made into a scavenger hunt game, and the children can look for pairs of items in the yard or playground, or around the house or classroom.

Pasta Puzzle

Purpose: This activity targets gross motor bilateral integration and increased proprioceptive and vestibular input for improved sensory motor processing. Allowing children to submerge their hands in a bowl of cooked noodles provides increased tactile input and an opportunity to describe novel sensations. This activity encourages children to take turns, request appropriately and share materials.

Materials: You will need a large piece of butcher paper and a bowl of cooked linguini noodles.

Description: Place a large piece of butcher paper on the floor. Map out a large picture in dot-to-dot format using numbers or letters, depending on the child's skill level. The picture depicted in the dot-to-dot activity can be as simple as a fruit or as complex as a tree, sun, house, or fish.

Depending on the teacher's artistic ability, he or she may opt for more complex patterns that can be found on the internet. Holiday dot-to-dots can also be found, such as pumpkins or holiday trees. Show the children where to place the first noodle and how to stretch it from the first position to the second position (if using letters, "A" to "B"; if using numbers, "1" to "2"). Complete the pattern by connecting all the dots to make a picture. If a noodle is too long and extends beyond the letter or number, pinch off the end so there is no excess. If the noodle is not long enough, encourage children to align the ends of the noodles so that they make a straight line.

Have the children describe how the noodles feel. They should appropriately request materials from each other, such as "Can I please have five noodles?" The children should crawl on their hands and knees and stretch their upper body to place the noodles on the paper. Encourage them to shift their weight to one side and cross the midline while retrieving noodles. Once all the noodles are in place, finish the picture by painting and decorating the paper.

Variations:

- To make this into a table-top activity, have the child make a shape—for example, a square—out of the noodles on a piece of paper. Continue placing noodles along the inside of the edge to fill in the shape. Different color noodles can be used to make a rainbow effect.

- Allow the children to have free play and create their own picture with the noodles.

Add food coloring to the water while boiling to make colored linguini noodles.

SIMPLY SENSORY

Fruity Greetings

Purpose: This activity provides the opportunity to practice working with eating utensils for increased fine motor control and independence with self-feeding. It promotes the development of hand–eye coordination. This activity provides an opportunity for labeling and following multi-stepped directions. It allows children to explore and express emotions and feelings, while discussing the special person for whom they are making the card.

Materials: For this activity you will need to cut whole apples into ¼–½ inch (0.5–1 cm) slices, large enough to use cookie cutters to cut out novel shapes. Determine what the occasion for the card is and choose appropriately themed cookie cutters, such as holidays, animals, or shapes. Place different color paints on a few paper plates and bowls. You will also need plastic forks, heavy weight construction paper, and a crayon or maker.

Description: Cut out shapes from the apple slices by using the cookie cutters. Place a couple of the apple shapes on the plates and in the bowls to ensure they are covered on one side with paint. Call on a child who is seated nicely and waiting his or her turn appropriately to choose which color he or she wants first. Describe the desired behavior, such as "I like how Maria is sitting quietly in her seat with her eyes on me." Ask the remaining children to choose a color; if a child is non-verbal, have him or her point to a picture of the color. Call on another child who is seated nicely and ask him or her to distribute the forks, while reiterating the desired behavior from that student.

Next ask children to choose a piece of colored construction paper, again choosing the child who is exhibiting desired behaviors to go first. Fold the piece of construction paper in half, and then half again, creating a card. Show the children how to use the forks to stab the apple slices and stamp them on the paper.

Discuss the purpose of the card and encourage the children to share who they are making the card for and why. Encourage the children to use feeling and emotion words when discussing their special person. For example, "My special person makes me feel happy when I am with them," or "I feel love for my special person." Continue to encourage the children to engage with each other, asking questions, and complimenting each other's work. Have each child sign their work.

Variations:

- A good alternative for children with weak grasp is to use corncob holders. Have them stab the apple slices using both hands to pick up the apple slice for stamping.

- Feel free to encourage children to add additional craft materials to their card, such as glitter, feathers, sticker, confetti, and much more.

 Old, large-sized, men's button-down shirts make great smocks to help keep the children's clothes clean.

Smell That?

Purpose: This activity explores the olfactory sense. Scents are commonly used to induce relaxation or alert emotional states. Discuss the properties of the scent and explore the child's likes and dislikes. This activity targets fine motor development by strengthening isolated finger control and facilitating bilateral integration. This is a good activity for improving hand–eye coordination and strengthening scissor skills. See the Appendix for list of descriptors.

Materials: You will need a range of aromatherapy oils. For eliciting a calming state try lavender, vanilla, jasmine, rose or sandalwood. To explore stronger scents with alerting characteristics try peppermint, rosemary, cedar wood, lime, or cinnamon. If these scents are not available, commonly found kitchen products can be used. For example, vanilla extract is a good calming scent, while lemon and peppermint extract and vinegar are alerting scents. You will also need cotton fabric squares, cotton balls, yarn, safety pin, and scissors. Older children with advanced fine motor skills can use a needle and thread.

Description: Cut out 4-by-4 inch (10 x 10 cm) cotton squares in fun patterned fabric. Have the children request their fabric of choice using descriptive language such as, "I want the blue one with the red flowers on it."

For younger children who are unable to safely use sharp needles, align two squares together and fold a quarter inch of fabric along the edge of one of the sides of the square. Cut small slits (just enough space to fit yarn through) into the edge of the doubled-over fabric about a quarter to half an inch apart from each other. Do this for each side of the square. Place a small-sized safety pin on the end of a long piece of yarn and have the child lace the yarn through the slits with the safety pin for three sides of the square, to create a pocket. Stuff cotton balls into the pocket. Have the children choose a scent they like and allow them to share why they like it. Does it remind them of something or somewhere? Then soak the cotton balls in a generous amount of chosen aromatherapy oils or extract. Continue lacing up the final side of the pillow and tie in a bow knot with the beginning piece of the yarn.

Variations:

- A tapestry needle has a duller tip than a sewing needle and will also work with lacing the yarn.

- For smaller children, use larger-sized squares with larger-sized slits along the sides and ask them to simply use their hands to lace up the pillow.

Explore the child's likes and dislikes for each scent. Explore the sensory response of a calming scent in a heightened emotional state.

Beanie Shapes

Purpose: This activity targets improved isolated finger control to develop a pincer grasp and improved motor planning. This is a great activity to teach pre-writing skills and promote functional grasping patterns. It provides increased tactile discrimination for improved sensory processing. It also allows for the opportunity to discuss bean qualities, such as small, oblong, flat, kidney shaped, smooth, spotted, or little, as well as different colors, and more. This activity targets identifying and labeling shapes and/or letters and numbers.

Materials: For this activity empty a couple of large bags of uncooked "16 bean soup" into a large bowl. You will also need construction paper and glue.

Description: This activity can be done in a group or individually. Have the children sort some of the beans from a large bowl, so that they must immerse their hands, providing increased tactile input. Discuss the categorizing characteristics while sorting the beans. Discuss how the beans feel. Cut out 4 foot by 4 foot (1 m^2) squares out of the construction paper.

Have the children glue beans along pre-drawn lines and/or the outline of a geometric shape or pattern. Examples of pre-writing strokes include: horizontal lines, vertical lines, diagonal lines, and circles. Shapes can be as simple as a square or fish, or more complex such as an octagon, flower, or sailboat.

Use one type of bean for each line or shape and discuss bean characteristics while gluing them on the page. Once the beans have dried, have younger children isolate their index finger and run their finger over the beans for improved motor planning. Have them blindfolded and ask them if they can determine the shape on the page by running their fingers along the path.

Variations:

- To increase the challenge, have the child spell out his or her name with one letter on each page. Once the glue has dried, ask him or her to arrange the letters in the correct order with eyes covered.

- For children who are over-stimulated by this type of tactile input, provide a spoon and ask them to scoop the beans out of the bowl.

Balloon Paddle

Purpose: This activity promotes hand–eye coordination and upper body bilateral integration. This is a language building activity that promotes improving processing speed. It helps children with labeling and develops the concept of categorizing.

Materials: To create a paddle you will need a handle; this can be made out of a tongue depressor, paint stirrer, ruler, or Popsicle stick. Attach the handle of choice to the back of a sturdy paper plate with packing tape or masking tape. You will also need a blown up balloon. It has been determined that punch balloons (without the rubber band) work the best, as they have just enough weight to project further in the air.

Description: Have the children sit in a circle on the floor or in chairs facing each other. Pick a theme and have the children label an item from that theme each time they hit the balloon. For example, if the theme is animals, each student must say a different animal each time the balloon comes to them while hitting it to return it across the circle. If a child cannot think of a new animal or repeats an animal that has already been used he or she is out.

Variations:

- Use an appropriate theme depending on the children's skill level. For younger children or cognitively impaired children, have them recite the ABC or name colors each time they hit the balloon.

- To increase the challenge for older children, ask them to generate words starting with a specific letter, or rhyming words, each time they hit the balloon.

- For children with poor gross motor control, provide them with physical assistance to ensure they are hitting the balloon.

 Encourage the children to be thinking of the theme even when it is not their turn, so that they are ready when the balloon comes to them.

Seasonal Sensory Play-Dough

Purpose: This is a sensory-rich activity that encourages associations between seasons and smell, increases tolerance for touch, sequencing, creativity, labeling, describing, hand strength and bilateral integration. See the Appendix for a list of descriptors.

Materials: Each season will have different smell associations and "special ingredient(s)." The base recipe is the same for all variations. Play-dough can be stored in an airtight container or bag. You will need 1 cup (150 g) of flour, half a cup (140 g) of salt, 2 tablespoons of oil, 1 tablespoon of cream of tartar, 2 tablespoons of the "secret ingredient" or 1 package of powdered drink mix, and 1 cup (240 ml) of boiling water.

Description: Pass a small amount of each ingredient, approximately half a teaspoon, to each student so that they can label, feel, smell, taste, describe, compare, and contrast them. Then bring out the "secret ingredient" and let students touch, taste, and guess the theme of the play-dough. Next, mix together flour, salt, oil, and the secret ingredient. Add the cup of boiling water. Mix well. Knead the mixture until it forms a soft dough. Students can describe what it feels and smells like.

An adult can help with adding the boiling water. Make sure the play-dough has cooled prior to kneading. Some variations may leave you with colored hands.

Try substituting baby oil for vegetable oil in the play-dough recipes. The smell is wonderful and your hands are baby soft. If you add vanilla extract, almond extract, or peppermint extract to your homemade play-dough recipes it will make the play-dough last longer, prevent mold growth, make it smell good, and give it a smoother texture.

Seasonal variations:

- Summertime

    1. Lemonade play-dough: One package of unsweetened lemon-lime powdered drink mix.

    2. Peanut butter and jelly play-dough: One package of grape powdered drink mix and 2 tablespoons of peanut butter.

    3. Strawberry shortcake play-dough: One package of strawberry powdered drink mix and one teaspoon of vanilla extract.

- Fall

    1. Pumpkin pie play-dough: One tablespoon pumpkin pie spice and one tablespoon cinnamon. Orange (yellow plus red) food color is optional.

    2. Apple pie play-dough: 1 teaspoon cinnamon, ½ teaspoon nutmeg, ¼ teaspoon allspice and ¼ teaspoon cardamom. Red food coloring is optional.

    3. Orange spice play-dough: One package orange powdered drink mix, 1 teaspoon cinnamon, 1 teaspoon ground cloves, ½ teaspoon ground ginger and ½ teaspoon ground nutmeg.

- Wintertime

    1. Wintermint play-dough: One teaspoon of toothpaste and/or a couple of drops of mint or peppermint extract.

    2. Snow play-dough: One tablespoon of glitter.

    3. Gingerbread play-dough: One tablespoon of ground ginger and one teaspoon of cinnamon.

    4. Hot cocoa play-dough: One tablespoon of cocoa and one teaspoon of vanilla.

    5. Red velvet cake play-dough for Valentine's Day: One package of raspberry powdered drink mix and one tablespoon of cocoa.

- Springtime

    1. 50–50 bar play-dough: One package orange powdered drink mix and one teaspoon vanilla.

    2. Grape ape play-dough: One package of grape powdered drink mix with a sprinkle of glitter.

    3. Cherries jubilee: One package of cherry powdered drink mix and a couple of drops of vanilla or rum extract.

Variations:

- Add texture with fish gravel, birdseed, coffee grounds, cornmeal, tea, glitter, sand, rice, beans, beads, etc.

- Make shapes like: ABCs, 123s, animals and flowers using cookie cutters or a plastic knife.

- Make the shape of the secret ingredient. For example, if the smell is pumpkin pie, the students can make the shape of a pumpkin.

Shaving Cream Rainbow

Purpose: This is a fun activity that provides increased proprioception and tactile input. It encourages children to use descriptor words for the texture, sensation, smell, and color of the shaving cream.

Materials: Place a generous amount of newspaper on an open space on the floor, ideally on tile or linoleum. Place a large-sized piece of butcher paper on the newspaper. Have the children squeeze shaving cream into four to six large bowls (depending on how many colors you use), then add generous amounts of food coloring. The children can use their hands or a spoon to stir in the color.

Description: Draw a large-sized rainbow on the paper. Have the children paint each section of the rainbow using their hands. Encourage them to crawl on their hands and knees and stretch while crossing midline to get to different parts of the rainbow. Discuss the way the shaving cream feels and smells. Discuss the properties of the primary colors. Discuss how you make orange, green, and purple. Encourage the children to share materials by modeling interactions, such as "Can I please have the red?" Encourage the children to comment on each other's work. Ask them to share their favorite color and why.

Variations:

- If the child is resistant to submerging their hands in the shaving cream, provide a paintbrush for them to use.

- Each student can make their own rainbow at their desk or at a group table; however, continue to encourage the children to ask each other for materials.

- Keep a towel handy to wipe hands and arms between colors. This is a great time to provide deep pressure to the hands, arms and shoulders with firm rubbing of the towel. Please be cautioned that the food coloring may temporarily stain the hands. Latex gloves can be used if this is an issue.

Skipping Stones

Purpose: This activity helps promote overall gross motor development and bilateral integration. It provides balance challenges as well as proprioceptive and vestibular input. This activity promotes problem solving and provides an opportunity for using inferences.

Materials: To create the stones you will need 10–12 phone books. Wrap the entire phone book in masking tape so that it is sturdy and rigid. You can wrap two or three phone books together to create a higher stone. You will need descriptors of items, either in picture form with Picture Exchange Communication System (PECs) cards or written on a note card, depending on the child's skill level.

Description: Arrange the stones into a path or straight line with the higher stones randomly interspersed within. Determine the best distance is to lay the stones according to each child's ability to jump with both feet from one stone to the next safely. At each stone have a clue for a mystery object they will get at the end of the path. Have the children collect the clues as they jump to each stone.

Once they arrive at the final stone have a number of items presented to them and ask them to choose the item they think the clues are referring to. For example, if a student collects the following clues: round, red, fruit, grows on a tree, the student can infer the item is an apple. This can be done at snack time with various foods.

Variations:

- For younger children, arrange the stones in a circle and assign a movement or activity to each stone with a visual or written label. For example, one stone could be the dancing stone, and another could be the humming stone or the wiggling stone. Have the children walk along the stones to music and, once the music stops, they can perform the action for that stone.

Ensure each student is wearing appropriate shoes, with the laces tied to decrease the risk of falling. For students with balance challenges, provide physical assistance as they navigate between stones.

SPEAK, MOVE, PLAY AND LEARN WITH CHILDREN ON THE AUTISM SPECTRUM

Sock Snake

Purpose: This activity helps improve grasping patterns and strengthens isolated finger control. It helps improve bilateral integration of the hands as well as hand–eye coordination. The snake provides increased proprioceptive input and can be used as a tool for self-regulation. This activity encourages following multi-stepped directions and sequencing.

Materials: The snake is made of simple materials commonly found in the household and classroom. You will need a new, long, cotton tube sock, a few bags of dried beans, large- and small-sized buttons, a piece of red fabric, scissors, and needle and thread or glue, depending on the child's skill level.

Description: For older children with developed fine motor skills and good safety awareness, have them sew two large buttons on the toe-end of the sock to represent eyes. Next, sew a smaller button on the sock for a nose. Take a piece of red fabric and cut it into the shape of a tongue and sew it in the appropriate place. Allow the children to decorate their snake with markers or stamps. Encourage the children to ask each other for materials using descriptor words and appropriate requesting. For example, "Can I please use the green glitter?" Place lots of beans into a large bowl. Have the children submerge their hands in the beans and describe how it feels. Have them scoop the beans with their hands or a large spoon into the sock, leaving a quarter of the sock empty. Tie the open end of the sock into a tight knot.

Variations:

- For younger children or children with less developed fine motor skills, use fabric circles for eyes and nose, and glue them on with fabric glue or a hot glue gun. This also reduces the risk of choking.

The sock snake can be used as a tool for self-regulation. For children who tend to enjoy squeezes or squishes, lay the snake over their shoulder. Squeeze their arms through the snake providing deep proprioceptive input. Children often use lap buddies or weighted lap sacks at school while seated at their desk to help them maintain a calm body.

SIMPLY SENSORY

75

CHAPTER 6

Cooking

Cooking is one of the most useful, motivating, and universal activities in which we can engage our students. It can be as simple or as complex as we would like it to be. Every student can be successfully involved in some kind of cooking activity. Cooking can be a work role, play or leisure activity, and even self-care. One can cook for oneself, cook for a family, or cook for groups of people—the possibilities are endless. Cooking is not only about preparing food. With just a little bit of planning, it can become much more than just a simple act of turning ingredients into a meal. Spending time with your children in the kitchen can be very rewarding for everyone involved. Not only is it fun, but there are many developmental benefits to having kids in the kitchen.

Given the enormous number of different ways in which cooking can be accomplished, it lends itself exceptionally well to many therapeutic applications. Participation and motivation to partake in cooking activities are always high for students and teachers. These are great groups that rarely fail.

Cooking together provides an opportunity to spend time together

We are always looking for opportunities to spend time together in a productive and fun way. Cooking is one of those activities that occurs daily, and involving your child in an active process of meal preparation is a great way to do it. It can be just you and your child or it can involve the whole family. Any time we cook with someone this activity automatically becomes a teamwork project. When involving siblings in cooking activities it is a wonderful way to promote the development of caring for each other and bonding. It promotes exchange of information and is a natural learning opportunity for everyone involved. Yes, we can learn a lot from our children.

Building memories

Because of the structure of our brain, smell often triggers memories, and we build new memories based on smells. Cooking is a multi-sensory experience of which smells are a big and inseparable part. Cooking together will promote the development of unforgettable memories. Also, it can bring back previous memories (i.e. cooking with Grandma last summer). Sharing with your children "secret" family recipes will further support the family bond.

Spending time in the kitchen will boost their confidence

We all need the feeling of being successful at doing something. This is especially true for children, who are always looking to prove themselves in our eyes. Giving them a chance to master a new skill is a sure way of bringing a huge smile to their faces. Learning how to feed oneself is an ideal way to boost self-esteem and teach responsibility. Even the smallest tasks, such as stirring a batter, will make them feel important.

Discovering new flavors

Many children are picky eaters and it is extremely hard to convince them to try some new foods. The chances of trying new flavors are greater if we involve children in the active process of food preparation. Increasing exposure to a variety of foods will increase their interest in trying them. The natural curiosity might be stronger than the previously established perception of "I do not like——" and they might actually try something new without our encouragement.

Lasting skills

Cooking is one of the essential skills that lasts a lifetime. It can become a skill that is used daily. By starting to develop it early we can greatly enhance chances for maximizing the potential of our children to be independent. Starting with small tasks in the kitchen will prevent discouragement.

Healthy eating habits

With all the advertisement and ease of obtaining fast-food, teaching kids healthy eating habits seems like an enormous task. Cooking together provides us with an opportunity that should not be missed. Those small steps can be a contributing factor in developing healthy eating habits that will last throughout their lives. It creates a natural environment in which to discuss nutrition and the differences between fresh and processed foods. In addition, meals prepared from scratch usually contain fewer calories, chemicals, and sweeteners than pre-made foods.

Sensory experience

Cooking is a multi-sensory experience. Not only do we look at what we are cooking, but we also taste it (is there enough sugar in the lemonade?), smell it (I think our cookies are done!), feel it (is the dough sticky?), and often listen to it (is the water boiling?). It is OK to break an egg on the counter, spill flour, or put fingers in a batter—it is all part of the learning process.

What else can be learned through cooking?

Fine motor skills, language, counting, fractions, budgeting, weighing, sequencing, measuring, problem solving, sharing, science, reading, using basic tools—these are just a few of the skills learned through cooking. So enjoy this wonderful chapter and go ahead, get your hands in the batter.

PBJ Sandwich Shapes

Purpose: To develop basic self-care, daily living skills, bimanual coordination, turn taking, sequencing, kinesthetic feedback, motor control, and cooperation.

Tools: Cookie cutters, butter knife, and plates.

Ingredients:

Sliced bread

Peanut butter

Jelly

Description: Participants should pair up. Each participant gets a plate, a knife (a butter knife is preferred), and two slices of bread. One student gets peanut butter, another jelly. They both spread one of them on both pieces of bread. Using a cookie cutter, the students cut shapes out of their slices of bread. Now, the fun part: both students match their shape to the corresponding shape of their partner (emphasize general design, as well as orientation and alignment) and magic happens. Each student will end up with a PBJ sandwich in a novel shape.

Don't forget to have students clean up after the project.

Variations:

- Increase the number of cookie cutters. The minimum for two students are four pieces of bread and one cookie cutter—the finished product will be two PBJ sandwiches (one for each student). You can increase the number of cookie cutters used, but remember that each shape needs a match for a PBJ sandwich.

- Try different spreads. You don't have to limit yourself to peanut butter and jelly. Depending on students' preferences, you can use different spreads (cream cheese, strawberry jam, Nutella®, sunflower seed butter (in case of allergies to peanuts), etc.) or go for a ham-and-cheese sandwich.

Taco Treat

Purpose: To develop new, expressive language and vocabulary, follow three- or four-step directions, sequencing, weight bearing, bilateral integration, cutting, rolling, attributes, hand strengthening, upper-body control and stretching.

Tools: Rolling pin or two plates, two ziplock bags, and a pan.

Ingredients:

Masa (cornmeal)

Water

Salt

Description: Masa can be found in most grocery stores under the Mexican Food section. To make the masa follow the directions on the bag. Most masa is simply made by just adding water and salt to the cornmeal. Have the student mix the cornmeal, water, and salt in a bowl until it becomes a dough. The masa can be kneaded by hand, and in fact this is the original way of making tortillas.

Get the dough and roll into 1 inch (2.5 cm) wide balls for little tortillas and 2 inch (5 cm) balls for regular-sized tortillas. Set the balls aside and get one ziplock bag. Cut two sides of the bag to form a folded piece of plastic that is attached by only one side. Place one ball on one side of the bag and then flip over the other piece of plastic bag to cover the ball. You will be left with a ball of masa between the plastic bag. Put the bag and masa ball on top of a plate and press down with another plate over it. Or you can use a rolling pin to roll out the masa ball into a tortilla. Remove the top piece of plastic and then peel off the tortilla.

Place the tortilla into a pan and cook on medium heat for about a minute on both sides. Throughout the process make sure to talk about how the dough feels between their fingers, how it smells, the color, texture, and make sure to teach the new words—such as tortilla, masa, rolling pin, and others—that the student might not know.

Variations:

- Use food coloring to add a cute touch and personalize the tortillas.

- Add butter and salt for a quick snack.

- Shred cheese and add to the tortillas to make quesadillas. The shredding incorporates more occupational therapy goals and vocabulary.

- Students can mash beans to add to the tortillas for tacos.

- Cut up slices of queso fresco, tomatoes, onions, cilantro, and avocado for a yummy salsa that can be added to the tacos.

Lotsa Pasta

Purpose: To learn new, expressive vocabulary, hand–eye coordination, bimanual coordination, labeling, sequencing, following multi-step directions, and fostering independent life skills.

Tools: Pizza cutter, bowl, fork, and rolling pin.

Ingredients:

3 cups (450 g) all-purpose flour

¾ cup (180 ml) water

1 teaspoon salt

Description: Have students put the flour in a mound on a large, floured surface or into a bowl and describe how the flour feels in their hands, how crumbly and white it is, and how soft it feels. Make a well in the center. They should follow the sequence to add the water and salt. Using their hands, they should gently work the water into the flour and continue until the dough becomes sticky and difficult to work with the hands. At this point you can compare and contrast the flour from before the water was added. Point out that the new flour and water combination is sticky and more solid than before.

Students should use their hands to form the rough dough into a ball. Let the dough rest for ten minutes. Knead the dough until it is smooth and elastic, for about ten minutes. Divide the dough into three or four balls and let rest for 30 minutes. Roll out one ball at a time to the desired thickness, and then use the pizza cutter to cut it into various shapes. Use long, thin strokes for fettuccine, thick strips for lasagna, and little squares for ravioli. You can have the students take their pasta home to share with their family for dinner or do one of the variations.

Variations:

- Assistive Technology (AT): Use a rocker adaptive knife or a universal cuff to help students who might have difficulty holding the tools.

- Shred cheese, cut mushrooms, spinach, or any other ingredient you wish to use to make different fillings for the ravioli and use a fork to press the ends of the ravioli together.

- For lasagna, layer your favorite fillings and top with cheese for a yummy dinner.

French Toast Fingers and a Thumb

Purpose: To develop bilateral coordination, strengthening, basic cooking skills, safety skills, olfactory awareness, sequencing, following simple directions, labeling, and describing.

Tools: Plastic knife, shallow bowl, whisk, measuring cup, measuring spoons, spatula, nonstick pan, or griddle.

Ingredients	Gluten free	Allergen free
¾ (180ml) cup milk		Soy milk
1 teaspoon vanilla extract		Real vanilla bean
5 eggs		Egg substitute or 3 mashed ripe bananas
½ teaspoon cinnamon		
¼ teaspoon nutmeg		
2 teaspoons sugar		Brown sugar or honey
¼ teaspoon salt		
2 slices of bread per student	Rice bread	
Cooking spray		Oil
Syrup		Maple syrup or apple sauce

Description: Introduce the ingredients and tools by letting each student touch, smell, taste, and label or describe them one by one. Then encourage the students to guess, "What are we making today?" After each student has made a guess reveal, "Today we are making French Toast Fingers and a Thumb." Read the following directions to the students to ensure good listening habits and ask questions about what was read. The student who has the answers gets to help with the first step.

Step 1: In a shallow bowl, whisk together all ingredients except the bread. Each student gets a turn at whisking the mixture.

Step 2: Pass out two pieces of bread to each student. One piece of bread represents the palm of the hand and the second piece of bread will get cut into four fingers and a thumb.

Step 3: Using a plastic knife, have each student cut a palm-shaped piece of bread and four fingers with a thumb. The students should describe each finger they have cut (thin, long, short, skinny, fat, thick, etc.), and compare it to the fingers on their hand.

Step 4: Dip both sides of the bread into the mixture, and cook in a lightly greased skillet over medium heat.

Step 5: When the cooking is finished, the students can arrange the bread on their plate in the shape of a hand. Add syrup and enjoy.

Variations:

• Prepare several toppings: syrup, powder sugar, fruit topping, peanut butter, etc.

• The instructor or a peer can dip a French Toast Finger into a topping and have the student identify the topping by taste. Students can close their eyes or simply turn away while the finger is dipped.

• Instead of whisking the ingredients into a bowl, try shaking them with a container that has a lid. The container can be passed to each student for a few seconds of shaking.

• Have students take turns being the sous chef by gathering ingredients and doing the basic preparation for the activity.

• Instead of fingers, use cookie or pizza cutters to make original designs from the bread.

To prevent the bowl from moving, place it on a damp towel.

Scissors are safer to use than a knife.

Fun Shaped Pancakes

Purpose: To develop hand–eye coordination, hand stabilization, naming shapes and letters, following multi-step directions, sequencing, and differentiating sizes (big, bigger, and biggest).

Tools: Measuring cup, spatula, nonstick pan, and pourable container.

Ingredients:

Water

Complete pancake mix, or gluten-free alternative, or allergen-free alternative

Description: Prepare the batter as directed on the box. Have one student read the directions on the box and someone else follow the directions as they are being read. Once the batter has been mixed pour it into a container with a pourable spout. Smaller spouts give greater control. Talk about the batter being a liquid and the container being a solid. You might also want to discuss how sticky, gooey and lumpy the batter is.

Heat the nonstick cooking pan to about 350°F (180°C). Have the children take turns making letters, shapes or pancakes of varying sizes. As the children wait for their letters or shapes to cook (about one-and-a-half minutes) ask them to name things that start with that letter or things that have the same shape as the one they are cooking. Use the spatula to flip the pancake and cook for about another minute. Ask some more questions about how the pancake smells, how it changed colors as it cooked, and how it changed from liquid to solid. Take the pancake off the pan and put it on a plate. Add syrup and enjoy.

Variations:

- Have a topping party where you provide lots of options for the toppings. Dare the students to try three different toppings before they add them to their pancakes. Some kids have an aversion to food but if we encourage them to taste different foods they might like them.

- Instead of syrup try using jam, honey, walnuts, pecans, pieces of fruit, compote, and Nutella. If there are nut allergies, use only fruit, jams, and honey.

- For more advanced students, have them make the pancakes from scratch.

- Have a contest to see who guesses two of your pancake shapes. The winner gets to eat them.

- Make pancakes of varying sizes and then sequence them from smallest to largest.

Salsa Snack

Purpose: To practice holding and cutting with a butter knife, labeling ingredients and tools, comparing and contrasting, and describing and using expressive vocabulary. This activity also helps with cultural awareness and teaching diversity.

Tools: Bowl, butter knife and cutting tablet.

Ingredients: All ingredients in this recipe are gluten free and nut free.

Traditional salsa	Alternative salsa 1	Alternative salsa 2
3 large tomatoes	3 large mangoes	3 large apples
½ medium onion	1 medium jicama	2 bananas
Cilantro (coriander) to taste	1 large cucumber	1 pint (24 medium) strawberries
½ lemon, squeezed	1 orange, squeezed	⅛ cup (30 ml) condensed milk

Description: The day before the activity have your students pick which type of salsa they want to make. Make a Pros and Cons table so that the students can compare and contrast the three different salsas and finally choose one they want to make. The salsas are ordered from sour to sweet with the traditional salsa being the least sweet and the fruit salsa being the sweetest.

On the day of the activity have all your ingredients on the table and ask your students to describe each one: how rough or smooth it feels, how fresh or crisp it smells, how hard or soft it is, what color it is, and how pungent.

Then have the students take turns cutting and dicing the items. Talk about "little" and "big" and "few versus many." The diced pieces should be put into the bowl. Make sure you go over prepositions like "in" and "out" as you go through this activity. For instance, you can say, "Put the cilantro in the bowl" or "Take the seeds out of the lemon."

Last but not least, squeeze either a lemon or an orange into your salsa or pour the condensed milk into the fruit bowl, depending on which salsa you are making. Have your students take turns doing the cutting and pouring. Then, when your food is done, have another student serve the food by asking, "Would you like some salsa?"

Variations:

- For students who need extra help holding the butter knife try hand-over-hand or an adaptive device.

- Play salsa music while the kids are cutting and eating the salsa. Have the kids do a dancing contest to see who is next to use the butter knife. Then the rest of the students keep dancing while someone cuts the food for a little while.

- For students who are not able to use a knife, even with an adaptive device, use a multi-purpose chopper such as the "Ultimate Chopper™" or the "Magic Bullet™."

- Use corn chips to scoop up some traditional salsa or spoon it on your tacos.

Don't dance too close to where the cutting is taking place. You might bump into the cutters and cause them to hurt themselves.

Refrigerate any unused portions and eat them at a later time.

Tres Leches Cake (Three Milks Cake)

Purpose: To develop describing, giving attributes, vocabulary building, in-hand manipulation, synonyms, antonyms, bilateral integration, sensory integration and hand–eye coordination.

Tools: Deep dish, or plate with 1-inch (2 cm) lip, variety of can openers, fork, and whisk.

Ingredients	Gluten free	Lactose free
1 angel food cake (sold at grocer's)	1 gluten-free angel food cake	1 angel food cake
1 (12 oz; 300 g) can evaporated milk	1 (12 oz; 300 g) can evaporated milk	1 can coconut milk
1¼ cup (300 ml) milk	1¼ cup (300 ml) milk	1¼ cup (300 ml) almond milk
¾ cup (180 ml) condensed milk	¾ cup (180 ml) condensed milk	¾ cup (180 ml) coconut cream
1 tbsp. vanilla extract	1 tbsp. vanilla extract	1 tbsp. vanilla extract
8 oz (200 g) whipped cream	8 oz (200 g) whipped cream	8 oz (200 g) lactose-free topping

Description: Take the angel food cake from its container and place it on the dish or plate. Explain how the lesson for today is going to be a Mexican recipe for tres leches cake. You can ask the children if they know anything about Mexico and they can use complete sentences to tell you what they know. You can also teach them that tres leches cake is eaten in hot places like Mexico because it serves as a cool and moist dessert.

To prepare the cake take volunteers who will help you open the cans. Make sure that you use different types of openers so that the children can learn how to open cans in many ways. Teach them how to punch holes in the hard lid of the can. Then have a student come up and make holes in the soft cake with a fork. Once done, have another student come up and pour the evaporated milk into a large bowl. Show how fast the milk pours. After this have another student pour the condensed milk into the same bowl. Point out how slowly this milk is pouring out. Last, pour the regular milk into the bowl. Add the vanilla extract at this time.

You can use a whisk to blend all the milks together. Try to use synonyms to describe the action of whisking; for instance, "mixing" and "beating." Compare and contrast all the aspects of the ingredients and the textures. Ask questions about colors, smells, sizes, shapes, and thickness of ingredients. Make sure that the holes you make with the fork on top of the cake are deep enough for the three milks to seep through. Once you have made all the holes, have a student pour the three milks mixture over the cake. Let it stand for 30 minutes while you set the table.

Once everything is set, cut the cake and make sure each child asks appropriately for a slice. Pick one of the students to be the whipped cream dispenser and have him or her go around asking everyone if they would like a squirt of whipped cream from the aerosol can. Enjoy!

Variations:

• You can teach Spanish words during the lesson. For instance:

uno—one dos—two tres—three leche—milk agua—water hola—hello adiós—bye amigo—friend pastel—cake sí—yes no—no más—more.

• You can add all kinds of fresh fruits to the cake. The tres leches cake is perfect for pairing with mango, peaches, and strawberries.

• For more advanced students you might want to explain how milk is condensed and evaporated. Then compare it to the water cycle (evaporation, condensation, precipitation).

COOKING

91

Lemonade

Purpose: The purpose of this activity is to develop hand/arm strength and hand–eye coordination, grasp, sequencing, describing, giving attributes, vocabulary building, bilateral coordination, and math (fractions) skills.

Tools: Knife, cutting board, plates, cups, pitcher or a jug if making one batch of lemonade, citrus juicer (any kind will work), and spoons.

Ingredients:

Lemons

Sugar

Ice

Chilled water

Optional: grenadine syrup, honey, raw/cane sugar

When making individual lemonades, one lemon per child is sufficient.

Description: Begin the activity by introducing the ingredients and tools. Allow the children to discuss the shape, color, and smell of lemons (scraping the outer skin helps release aromatic oils). If using different juicers, let the children describe how they work (electric, manual, push and turn, squeeze, etc.).

Distribute the plates (if not using a cutting board) and cups. Children should take turns cutting lemons in half.

The next step is to squeeze juice out of the lemons. Depending on the type of juicer being used, if any, techniques will vary, but in general it is easier to do it standing up at a table. Each child should collect juice from his or her lemon in a cup. When the squeezing part is done, encourage children to describe the juice—its taste, smell, and color.

The next step is to add sugar. Two teaspoons should be enough. Using spoons, stir the liquid to dissolve the sugar. Ask children to taste it and describe how it compares to pure lemon juice (more sweet, the same, or too sweet). Have children take turns adding water to their cups, leaving about a third of the cup empty for ice. Stir again, making sure all the sugar has dissolved. Ask children to taste their lemonade again and, if necessary, add some more sugar. The next step is to add some ice. While the lemonade is chilling in cups, have children help with cleaning up. The final step is to enjoy the lemonade.

Variations:

- Instead of using sugar, try honey.

- Adding some grenadine syrup will create "pink lemonade."

- When making one batch of lemonade, right after adding the water to the cups, have the children pour the contents of their cups into a jug or pitcher.

 Limit how much sugar children put in their lemonade. Two teaspoons per cup should be enough.

 Let the students taste, eat a piece of lemon, or drink the lemon juice. It won't hurt them and will provide them with a rich, sensory experience.

 A plastic knife works fairly well on ripe lemons.

English Muffin Pizza

Purpose: To develop bilateral coordination, strengthening, basic cooking skills, safety skills, sequencing and following simple directions.

Tools: Knife, spoon, small bowls/containers, microwave/toaster oven/ regular oven, plates, and spatula.

Ingredients:

English muffins

Pizza sauce

Shredded cheese

Toppings: pepperoni, olives, pineapple, bell peppers

Description: Arrange all the toppings in separate bowls. Have the children describe the toppings. Have them say which ones they like and which ones they dislike. Ask them to tell you which toppings are red, yellow, or black. After that, present each child with a plate and one slice of a muffin. Ask the kids to describe the inside of the muffin. Then have them compare the outside of the muffin with the inside. See who is behaving well and let that child be the first to get the pizza sauce.

Have the child spread pizza sauce on the muffin. Then talk about the different kinds of cheese there are. Have the kids sprinkle cheese on top of their muffin piece. Then allow the kids to ask for their toppings with full sentences. Let them add toppings. Bake for five minutes at 350°F (180°C) or microwave for one-and-a-half minutes.

Variations:

- Have the child cut toppings into smaller pieces.

- Instead of using shredded cheese, use a cheese grater to shred a chunk of cheese.

- Have the child use toppings to make "pizza faces"—happy, sad, angry, etc.

Lining the oven with aluminum foil makes cleaning up much easier.

Use extreme caution around the cheese grater and oven!

Crunchy Banana Cookies

Purpose: This activity provides a neat tactile experience while following multi-stepped directions, and you also make a delicious snack. It's a great activity for hand strengthening and bilateral integration and exploring the concepts of soft versus crunchy.

Tools: Knife, plastic bag, and plate.

Ingredients:

Ripe bananas

Graham crackers

Description: Ask the children to peal the banana. Discuss the identifying factors of the fruit; for example, "it is yellow," "it is long and round," or "it is soft." Have each child cut the banana into 1 inch pieces. Set the banana pieces aside.

Have the children crunch some graham cracker squares in their hands, into a bag, or onto a plate. Encourage the children to discuss how it feels.

Have the children put the remaining crackers inside a quart-size (one liter) ziplock bag and ask them to use their palms to crumble the crackers.

Once the graham crackers are finely crushed, have the children place one slice of banana into the bag. Tell them to shake up the bag and cover the banana with the crackers. Continue this process for the remaining banana slices. Discuss the concept of soft versus crunchy.

Variations:

- Other coating ingredients can be used as well, such as various kinds of cereals, oatmeal, or powdered sugar.

- Explore with various fruits and vegetables, discussing their quality and features.

For younger children or cognitively impaired children, a fork can be used to cut through the banana.

Fun-Do

Purpose: To discriminate between different flavors, compare and contrast scents, textures, flavors and colors, to discern attributes and descriptions from the items at hand, to practice pincer grasp and learn how to manipulate a fondue stick. They will also be cutting with a knife.

Tools: Wooden skewers, plastic knife, four bowls per table or group, fruit bowl, and cutting board.

Ingredients:

Fruity fun (gluten free)	Lactose free
Strawberries	Strawberries
Grapes	Grapes
Pieces of mango	Pieces of mango
Milk chocolate syrup	Dark chocolate syrup
Apricot jam	Apricot jam
Condensed milk	Strawberry jam
Grape jelly	Grape jelly

Description: This activity is a play on fondue but without the heated dangers of a real fondue.

Put a little apricot jam, condensed milk, chocolate syrup, and grape jelly in each of four bowls and place them in the middle of the table. Have the children label all the fruits on the table, describe the fruits by their attributes, and place them on a cutting board.

Instruct the kids how to cut the fruits into small pieces and then place all the fruit pieces into a bowl. Give each child a wooden skewer and give them some safety advice.

Working with plastic knives and skewers can be dangerous if the children are playing around and not following directions. Make sure you give a safety lecture and have a no-tolerance attitude. If kids play around with their skewers they lose their privilege and have to use forks instead.

Now comes the fun part. Have a child pick a fruit from the fruit bowl and then dip their fruit into one of the bowls with the syrup or jams. Once they take a bite of their dipped fruit ask them to describe the flavors. Have the kids try different combinations of fruits and dips until they find their favorite. This is a fun activity on a hot day because the fruit is very juicy and cooling.

Variations:

- Have the kids use different things to dip instead of fruit. They can try marshmallows with all kinds of flavored dips like strawberry syrup, caramel syrup and table cream.

- If you want to make this into a meal, try using deli cuts and meats and dip them into nacho cheese, bean dip, or hummus, while sausages can be dipped into different types of mustards.

- If the kids can't handle a skewer, use forks instead, but part of the purpose of this activity is to use one hand to skewer items and the other to hold the skewer.

Cupcake Match Up

Purpose: Kids will learn to copy sequences, recognize patterns, learn descriptive words, follow multi-stepped directions, use modeling to achieve the same results, use a pincer grasp, place items in specific places, have fine motor practice, and cross the midline.

Tools: Plates.

Ingredients:

Candy cupcakes	Gluten-free cupcakes	Candy-free cupcakes
24 undecorated cupcakes	Gluten-free cornbread	24 undecorated cupcakes
Chocolate sprinkles	Chocolate sprinkles	Coconut shavings
Rainbow sprinkles	Rainbow sprinkles	Coconut shavings
Coloring		
M&Ms®	M&Ms	Raisins
Candy corn	Candy corn	Dried cranberries
Heart candies	Heart candy	Banana chips
Skittles®	Skittles	Walnuts
Frosting (one color)	Frosting	Heavy whipping cream

Description: The object of this game is to get the kids to line up the same decorations on their cupcakes by using your cupcake as the model. This is a variation of a popular computer game where you have to have the same pattern on the cake as the computer's pattern. The children will have to listen to the teacher as he or she ices the cupcake, and then places a specific pattern on the cupcake top by using the candies from the candy bank (a plate where all the candies are kept).

After the teacher finishes his or her cupcake the students have to copy it and use the exact same pattern of candies on their cupcakes. If they did a great job then the teacher can pick them to be next to model a new patterns. They can make up their own patterns and have the other students follow them step by step, or for harder challenges have the kids wait until the end and then do the pattern. This will test their memory.

Variations:

- Have the kids do a very simple sequence and then, as they get more practice, have them do patterns of up to eight different toppings.

- Arrange the patterns in a way that seems significant to beginners. For instance, try making faces with hair or turning the cupcakes into animals. This is easier for them to follow.

- For more advanced students, have them start off with a variety of frostings. For instance, you can have a chocolate frosting base and then do fruit toppings. Or do a green frosting base and add candies. This way they have to keep track of frosting colors and toppings.

- Sell the cupcakes at a bake sale, or during lunchtime for some social pragmatics practice. Have the students greet everyone that comes to buy.

- Make the candy bank very diverse so that the kids have to sort out their candies or fruit before they begin to make out the pattern.

- Invite friends over during lunchtime and have a cupcake feast where the children can practice conversation skills with other students. See if they can use their words to describe the patterns on their cupcakes or how they managed to copy the patterns onto the cupcakes.

- You can use all fruit if you don't want to use candies, and if you don't have any nut allergies use walnuts, pecans, pine nuts, and cashews.

Shake It!

Purpose: Shake It! provides students with sensory feedback to the hands, wrists and arms. It is a functional alternative to flapping. Describing, labeling, motor coordination, sequencing and activities of daily living are all targeted in these easy, really fun activities.

Tools: Various sizes of ziplock bags, covered bowls or cups, and an assortment of cooking utensils.

Ingredients: For details, see the activities below.

Description: Place the desired ingredients in a bag or covered bowl and shake. Don't forget to label and describe all the ingredients. Verbally sequence each variation and have the students repeat for clarification. Ask questions and encourage interactions.

To create even more motivation and discussion, use clear plastic containers so that the students can observe what is happening inside.

Activities:

Shake Your Butter: A super popular activity with children and adults. I do this at least twice a year and get cheers every time.

Simply put a quarter cup (60 ml) of heavy whipping cream into a plastic cup with a lid. Add a sprinkle of salt if desired. Observe and describe the color and consistency of the liquid at this time. Cover tightly and begin shaking fast at first, then faster and more and more vigorously.

After about two minutes, when no liquid can be heard sloshing around, have students remove the lid and again describe the consistency. Maybe even let them have a small taste. Replace the lid and shake again and again, for between five and seven minutes. When liquid can be heard in the container, shake for one more minute. Have students count down the minute or watch the clock. Now, take off the lid and describe the contents.

There should be a watery liquid (buttermilk) and a solid (butter). Students should be encouraged to try the buttermilk, describe the taste and then spread the butter on a favorite cracker or piece of toast.

Shake Your Ice Cream: A fantastic summer, sensory, yummy and motivating activity. You will need per student:

I pint ziplock, storage bag (570 ml)

I gallon-size ziplock, storage bag (4.5 liters)

Ice cubes

$^{1}/_{3}$ cup (80 ml) rock salt

I tablespoon of sugar

$^{1}/_{2}$ cup (120 ml) milk

$^{1}/_{4}$ teaspoon vanilla

Chocolate or strawberry flavors (optional)

Take a shortcut and use half a cup of pre-made, flavored milk in vanilla, chocolate and strawberry. For individuals who do not tolerate dairy products, use soy, almond, rice, or coconut milk. Add milk, vanilla, and sugar to the small plastic bag and zip up. Double check that the bag is zipped closed. Fill the large bag half full of ice and add a third of a cup of rock salt. Place the small bag into the large bag and zip. Double check that zip again. Shake for five to six minutes. When the milk has turned into a solid, remove the small bag and enjoy your treat.

This is a great activity to talk about solids and liquids via the ice/water and milk/ice cream. Students can compare and contrast the salty taste of the rock salt and the sweet taste of the sugar. Students can also speculate why rock salt is needed to make ice cream. Hint: It drops the freezing temperature of the water to below the freezing point.

Shake Your Pudding Paint (Edible): Yum yum! Colorful pudding paint or finger-paint is guaranteed to be easy and fun. All you need are three simple ingredients:

3.4 oz (100 g) instant vanilla pudding

2 cups (480 ml) cold water

Food coloring

Divide the pudding mix equally into four small, cup-sized containers with lids. Add half a cup (120 ml) of cold water and a few drops of food coloring to each container, place the lid on tightly, and shake. Students can also choose colors and how many drops to add for bright or pastel.

COOKING

101

The instructor can take the opportunity to talk about consistencies, measuring, color mixing, and quantities like "more" and "less." Verbal sequencing and following directions can be easily targeted while making pudding paint. Students can now paint their masterpieces or use their fingers to create works of art and instructors enjoy peace of mind knowing there are no toxins in this paint.

Shake Your Salad: Mix your own salad quickly and mess free. This is a fun way to get your students to eat more fruit and/or vegetables, or at least touch and smell them. You will need one medium bowl with a top for each student and an assortment of fruit, vegetables, nuts, cheese, croutons, dressings, etc. Students can label each ingredient and describe the smell, taste, and texture. Then they can choose their favorite ingredients and how much they want in their bowls. Next, add two tablespoons of dressing, cover, and shake. Delicious! Even the pickiest eaters enjoy the process and usually try a bite or two.

Shake Your Trail Mix: Trail Mix is a practical way to get students to eat a more nutritious snack. It is a fun finger food that can be thrown into a backpack or lunchbox and encourages healthy eating choices. The best part of Trail Mix is that anything goes. Mix together desired portions of nuts, cereal, seeds, dried fruit, mini marshmallows, chocolate chips, etc. in a ziplock bag or re-sealable container and shake.

Don't forget to label, describe, taste, smell, and categorize all ingredients prior to making the Trail Mix. Students can practice opening and closing re-sealable containers as well as measuring ingredients while making Trail Mix.

Shake Your Morning Eggs: Scrambled eggs are a fantastic breakfast or anytime meal. They are high in protein, super healthy, and can be combined with many ingredients that kids love. Just the egg itself is a whole language and sensory lesson. Start with describing the outside and guessing what is inside. Talk about the texture of both raw and cooked eggs.

Let the students break an egg into a small sealable bowl.

Raw eggs can have bacteria so make sure to wash hands after cracking the egg.

Next, add your favorite ingredients: cheese, salt, pepper, chives, salsa, etc. Be sure to taste, smell, prepare and describe each ingredient prior to adding to the egg. After all the ingredients are in the bowl, put the lid on and shake for one to two minutes. Cook with low heat on a stovetop or for two to three minutes in the microwave, using a microwave-safe container. Serve with toast or muffins, or eat plain. Take time to talk about the texture and color of the eggs after cooking.

Variations:

- Have your students shake anything shakable, like salad dressing, whipped cream, juice mixes, etc. This is a functional alternative to flapping.

- Students can have fun while shaking by calling out ways to Shake It! For example: Shake It fast, Shake It slow, Shake It like a Polaroid picture, Shake It left or Shake It right.

- Shake it while singing the Hokey Pokey or any other fun, fast-tempo song.

CHAPTER 7

Artistry

One essential characteristic of all people is a drive to create. We create objects that are useful and make our daily lives easier, but we also create things that have no apparent usefulness. They do not make our daily tasks easier, they do not directly increase the quality of our work, and nor do they improve our work efficiency. Art has always been an integral part of human lives. As much as we like to look, listen, touch, and admire others' works of art, they have the most remarkable value to their creator. The process of creation—be it a poem, song, sculpture, or painting—provides opportunity for self-expression in a form that otherwise would not be achievable.

Research confirms the important role of artistry in development of self-confidence (Karlstad 1986): artistry creates a bridge between "I can't" and "I did it." Because there are no limitations on how art should be created, anyone can be involved. Another factor that makes artistry so appealing is the minimal requirement of tools and materials—in most cases, any household already has sufficient supplies for a great art project.

Artistry is not just a means of developing self-expression. Through engagement in art projects, students improve fine motor, perceptual motor, visual attention, eye–hand, sequencing, social, language, and myriad other skills. When engaging our students in an art project, there is one important thing to remember: the ultimate goal is not the final project, but the process of creation.

Safari Search

Purpose: To develop giving and following directions, pre-writing skills, drawing simple shapes, new expressive vocabulary, symbolic play, categories and cutting.

Materials: For this activity you will need paper, tape, and either crayons or markers, or colored pencils.

Description: The first thing you should do is to ask the students to name some African animals. Ask them to draw the basic shapes that form the safari animals and then have them color in their animal.

Talk about which animals have stripes, spots and fur, which ones are big, and which ones are little. For more advanced students, discuss which animals are predators and which are prey.

Once they have done their drawing, have them cut out the animal and tape it up somewhere in the room. The students can then take turns leading the class to the part of the room where their animal is displayed by giving verbal directions. The class follows the student's orders until they can "catch" the animal in their safari. This goes on until everyone has had a turn to lead and follow the safari.

Variations:

• Have the children make hats for going on safari the day before.

• The students can also use two toilet-paper rolls taped together with a long string attached to create binoculars for the safari hunt.

• The safari can be done around the entire school for more advanced students. And for more detailed directions, they can even draw a map to their animal and have the students follow the trail. Or you can print out copies of the school map and have the students draw the trail to their animal.

• To encourage turn taking, have the safari guide lead a few expeditions to see the animals but on the last one say, "Oh no, the tour guide let his or her tourists get eaten by the lion," or by the animal that they were following. At this point you can pick a new tour guide.

Edible Jewelry

Purpose: To develop hand–eye coordination skills, prehension (grasp) skills, sequencing skills, number sense, comparing and contrasting, order and magnitude, and following directions.

Materials: You will need string (yarn or thread), scissors, and pieces of paper to use as placemats, as well as cereal rings (such as Cheerios®) of many different flavors—for example, banana, chocolate, cinnamon, and apple.

Description: Have the children sit at a table where there are placemats, one for each child. Bring out the regular cereal rings and have the children take turns describing what they look like. Try to get words like circle, round, rough, little, spotted, and color descriptors. When a child gives you an answer, pour a few cereal rings onto their placemat. Do this with the other varieties, making sure that they are describing, and then comparing and contrasting, the different colors, shapes, and smells of the cereals.

Once everyone has at least three kinds of cereal on their placemats you can cut them a piece of string, longer than necessary. Tie one of the cereal rings to one end of the string to prevent the rest from falling off the end. Alternatively, you can secure the string to the table with a piece of tape. Have the child string enough cereal pieces on to make a sufficient length for a bracelet or a necklace. If necessary, remove the first cereal ring (the one that was tied to the end of the string) so that you can easily tie both ends of the string securely to create a closed loop. Enjoy the new necklace as a fashion accessory or as a take-along snack!

Depending on the skill level of the child, you might want to assist him or her in stringing cereal rings. Alternatively, you can demonstrate the activity first or work on individual projects simultaneously.

Variations:

- Make a string with a sequence of different flavored cereal rings. Have your students copy the sequence or tell them step by step how to copy it. The more advanced the student, the trickier the sequence.

- Play music while the children work on their strings. They can get their mouths moving to an upbeat song or work quietly to a relaxing, instrumental CD at the end of the day.

- Have a contest to see who can make the same necklace as the one you made. The winner gets the necklace you made. Check that it is the same sequence.

- Blindfold kids and have them guess what flavor they are eating. Have them explain what they taste and then choose the flavor they think they have.

 When using yarn, it is often difficult to put it through a small hole. Use a piece of self-adhesive tape to make the end of the yarn stiff and easier to thread.

 To keep this project safe, especially when making a necklace, choose a string or yarn that can be easily broken without any tools.

Noodle Painting

Purpose: To develop fine motor skills, prehension (grasp) skills, hand–eye coordination skills, dexterity skills, sequencing, following simple directions, labeling and describing, and color concepts—primary (red, blue, yellow) versus secondary colors (orange, green, violet).

Materials: For this activity you will need old newspapers, paper plates or shallow bowls, paper sheets to paint on, and finger paint (or tempera for an easy clean-up), as well as cooked pasta—spaghetti works best.

Description: Cover the work surface with old newspapers. Introduce the materials by letting each child touch, smell, taste, label, and/or describe how spaghetti or paint feels. Encourage a discussion about shapes (plates and bowls are round, spaghetti is long with a round cross-section). Depending on the colors used, talk about primary versus secondary colors. When working with primary colors, encourage children to predict what will happen when they mix different colors. Reinforce the color concept by playing a game, such as asking them to name five things that are red (or yellow, blue, and so on).

Have children describe how spaghetti feels. Is it dry and stiff, or wet and moist? Is it hard or stretchy?

Put a little of each paint on separate plates. Have children get one noodle each and, holding it between thumb and index fingers, roll, drag, and twist it through the paint.

After the noodle is covered with paint, ask the children to transfer it to a clean sheet of paper and repeat the process of rolling, dragging, and twisting. Repeat this process until a sufficient amount of the required color is painted on the paper.

Ask the children to switch the plates with paint on so that each of them will get a different color. Repeat, adding a second, and then a third color to the painting.

After achieving a completed painting, have the children assist with the clean-up and proudly display their artwork.

Variations:

- Yarn, twine, ribbon, string, rope, or any kind of thick thread works well for this project—try different materials to achieve different effects.

- Little fingers sometimes have trouble holding the spaghetti—using a clothes pin or binder clip makes holding it easier.

- To work on secondary colors, provide children with plates that have two primary colors on them, allowing children to experiment with creating "new" colors.

Quick color-mixing ideas:

red + yellow = orange

yellow + blue = green

red + blue = violet

This activity can be messy—you can never have too many newspapers to cover the work area.

Chinese Dragon or Nordic Water Serpent

Purpose: This activity reinforces asking for items, identifying colors and shapes, tying knots, gluing, grasping, cutting, using a hole puncher, cutting with scissors, and developing sentences to tell a story.

Materials: You will need paper tube rolls, glue, yarn, colored construction paper, and a hole puncher.

Description: Kids love dragons and mythical creatures, and in this activity they get to create their very own Chinese dragon. First the teacher should ask if anyone knows what dragons are. After getting answers from the students fill in any cultural aspects they may have left out. For instance, you might want to add that dragons are considered by many cultures to be a symbol of good luck, power, and strength.

During the discussion, every time a student participates by saying something or answering a question you can reward them by giving them a tube roll. Each child should end up with three or four tubes.

Next, have the students ask for the hole puncher and make two holes at each end of the tube (four per tube) in a way that will make it easy to tie the tubes together when placed end to end (as in the picture below).

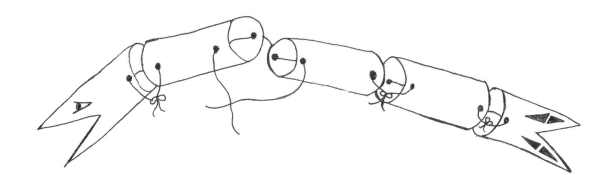

Next, have the students cut pieces of yarn long enough to tie the tubes together to form a long snake dragon. After you have formed a dragon, cut one of the ends of the tubes to make the head. Make two triangular cuts to form a gaping mouth on the dragon. Make sure that you make the holes on this tube behind the mouth, as in the picture above. To these

110

two holes attach a long piece of yarn that will be used to pull the dragon through the air.

Last but not least, cut pieces of colored paper to decorate the dragon. Now your kids are ready to pull their dragon through the winds or on the floor. The kids love the articulated parts because they make the dragon wiggle in a very lifelike way. After some time has been given to playing with their dragons, have the students take turns making stories about them.

Variations:

- For beginners, use paper tube rolls painted with acrylic paints and big brushes that are easy to grasp. They can use plastic ties to bind the articulated tubes together if they can't tie a knot.

- If the student cannot make up a story about their dragon, ask them to describe their dragon to you or another person.

- For intermediate students, cover the tubes with colored construction-paper pieces that are big enough to cover the entire length of the tube. They can decorate this paper with crayons or markers to make them more original.

- For advanced students, have them cut out individual scales about half an inch (1 cm) long and then have them glue each scale to the tubes. This is painstakingly difficult but a good challenge for them.

- The stories can be anything from a simple sentence such as "My dragon loves cookies," to entire stories with more than three parts. If your child can do it, have him or her type up a story.

- For cultural dynamism you can change the Chinese dragon to a Nordic water serpent.

ARTISTRY

"Who Am I?" Collage

Purpose: To develop awareness of the self, be able to describe yourself in new terms, use fine motor skills, grasping, master scissor skills, use expressive language, and learn presentation skills.

Materials: You will need printouts from the computer, pictures, magazines, glue, scissors, and large sheets of paper.

Description: This activity can begin with a brief discussion on what makes us who we are. Have the students give you answers to the question "Who am I?" Answers will vary but make sure to include very broad perspectives—for instance, humans, earthlings, members of the Milky Way Galaxy—and also very narrow perspectives such as Japanese, volleyball player, guitar soloist, and my name. Write down all these answers on a board so that you are also using visual aids.

After the discussion give the students a chance to go to the computer and print out images that help to describe who they are as people. Also allow them to look through magazines and cut out the symbols and pictures that call to them. If they prefer to draw something instead of cutting a picture that is also an option.

After about 30 minutes of gathering materials have the students cut and paste the pictures onto a large piece of paper. Once finished with the collage go over a few rules for presenting. Remind them to keep good eye contact with the audience, to speak loud enough for the people in the back of the room to hear, remind them not to cover their mouth with their paper, and tell them to try to breathe slowly and talk slowly. Finally, allow the students to present their collages to the rest of the class. Give everyone a round of applause for a great job.

Variations:

- If there are no magazines or computer printers available the students can always draw on paper.

- Have the students work on these collages over many days to make them more interesting and in-depth.

- Have the students take their collages home and give their parents a presentation too. Have the parents return a signed slip and reward the students with extra-credit goodies.

- For younger children, show them a magazine and have them cut out, as best they can, what attracts them. These may be their favorite toys or preferred food items. Then have them glue the images for a "Favorites collage."

Paper "Me Dolls"

Purpose: To master paper-cutting skills, manipulating tools, following three-step directions, developing creativity, nurturing self-awareness, discovering "me" words, using descriptors and naming attributes.

Materials: You will need copies of the "Girl outline" and "Boy outline" (these are in the Appendix)—one copy for each child—pencils, markers or crayons, and scissors.

Description: Begin a discussion about what makes us unique on the outside. The way we look, the way we dress, the ways we walk and carry ourselves are all good indicators of the person we are on the outside. Have the children discuss things we can add to our bodies, such as clothing preferences, shoe styles, and hat or beanie options. Then have them discuss things that are on the outside of their bodies that they were born with, like hair color, eye color, freckles, curly or straight hair, long legs, short stubby fingers, etc.

Now hand out a copy of the "Girl outline" or "Boy outline" to each child. The first step is for the children to draw on the features that make them unique. After they have finished drawing, hand them an extra piece of paper. The second step is to make clothes for their doll. They will, more than likely, need help to make and cut the clothes they draw.

Once everyone has dressed their "Me doll," the third step is to give each kid a chance to explain to the class what they did to make their doll and what it means to them. After everyone has shown their doll, make sure to thank them all for being so open with each other and sharing themselves.

Variations:

- Make this project a semester-long activity. Have the children lay on butcher paper and have their silhouettes drawn and cut out. Hang the dolls on the wall around the classroom. Then each week they can add something to their Me doll. On Valentine's Day they can add a heart with the names of people they love inside it. On Thanksgiving they can add three things they are thankful for.

- You can get creative and use things like glitter, feathers, yarn for hair, and other materials to make a more fun Me doll.

- Make a future Me doll. Have the kids build a doll of what they want their future selves to be and to look like. Have a list of careers ready for them to choose from.

Fuzzy Sheep

Purpose: To develop hand–eye coordination skills, grasp skills, sequencing skills, number sense, describing, using attributes, and labeling.

Materials: You will need a sheet of paper, crayons or markers, scissors, glue, cotton balls, and sandpaper, as well as sugar, rice, spices, and dry beans.

When using rice or dry beans, it is better to use liquid glue (i.e. Tacky glue), as opposed to stick glue.

Description: Ask the children what the difference is between sheep and goats. Have them compare and contrast the two animals. Using crayons or markers, draw the outline of a sheep on the paper. Ask the kids if they want a big or little sheep to guide your drawing. Ask if they want horns that stick up or are curved. Fill the "body" of the sheep with glue and attach cotton balls. Have the children guess how many cotton balls it will take to fill in the sheep drawing.

Continue filling out the separate parts of the picture with glue and the other desired materials. These materials could include: rice, to be used as small rocks, or dry beans for large ones; sandpaper as sand; dry parsley as grass; clear plastic wrappers as water; real leaves collected during a walk outside as trees, etc. Sandpaper can be torn into little pieces or desired shapes before gluing it to the picture.

Variations:

- You can provide the children with an already made drawing, in which case they just need to glue on the different materials.

- Alternatively, the children can be provided with partially made drawings and will need to finish the drawings themselves before gluing.

- When working with a group of children, each one can create a picture of a sheep in a different environment, i.e. lake, mountains, prairie, desert, forest, etc.

Cutting sandpaper with scissors is a great activity when teaching scissors skills to children, as it provides them with additional sensory feedback during cutting.

Small objects, such as dry beans, can be a choking hazard to children prone to placing objects in their mouths.

ARTISTRY

115

Coiled Creature

Purpose: To develop scissor-using skills, hand–eye coordination, bilateral integration, visual-motor skills, prehension (grasp) skills, sequencing skills, and following simple directions.

Materials: You will need bright markers or crayons, a paper plate, yarn or string, a hole puncher, and glue.

Description: Start the activity by providing each child with one paper plate and make markers/crayons available for use. Ask your students to color both sides of the plate. There are no rules for this part, so encourage creativity.

Starting on the outside of the plate, have students cut in a circular pattern, gradually spiraling toward the center of the plate. Each student should end up with a long "apple peel" spiral. Allow students to choose the thickness of their snake. If necessary, use a marker to provide a cutting line for a student.

Students can choose either to draw the head of the snake (center part of the plate) or use another plate to draw and cut out the head and a tongue. If the students choose to make a separate head/tongue, use glue to attach them to the body of the snake. Using a hole puncher, have students make a hole near the head—this is where the yarn will go to hang the snake up.

Variations:

- Plates can be decorated using glue and glitter, or they can be painted.

- A jingle bell or any other small bell can be attached to the snake's tail to create a rattlesnake. To do it, punch another hole at the tail end and tie a bell to it using a piece of yarn.

These snakes will really come to life when hung outside in a little wind.

Provide additional supervision during the final stage of cutting out the snake, as the holding hand will be very close to the scissors.

Personal Puzzle

Purpose: This activity promotes improved fine motor, bilateral integration, and visual-motor skills. It encourages the development of various visual perception skills, such as visual discrimination, spatial orientation, and visual closure. It promotes storytelling of personal information and experiences, such as how many brothers and sisters a child has, or a trip to an amusement park.

Materials: To make the photo puzzle ask the children to bring a few photos from home depicting family members, pets, a family vacation, or an extra-curricular activity the student engages in. Ensure the photos are copies and not originals. You will also need cardstock, scissors, and permanent markers.

Description: Glue the photo onto a piece of cardstock. Then use scissors to cut around the edges of the photo so the cardstock and photo are the same size. With a permanent marker draw a puzzle pattern on the photo. Have the children cut along the lines to make puzzle pieces of the photo. Mix up the pieces and have the children rearrange the photos.

Have the children discuss the photos. Encourage them to generate as much language as possible. However, if someone is struggling, encourage their peers to ask questions about the picture—for example, "Who is standing next to you?" or "What is your dog's name?".

Variations:

• Adjust the cutting difficulty according to the child's skill level. Straight lines are easiest to cut while numerous curves and corners are more difficult.

• To increase the challenge, mix two or three photos together.

 For children with basic scissor skills, use self-opening scissors to help develop hand movement.

Watercolor Initials

Purpose: To develop visual attention to task, prehension (grasp), sequencing, fine motor skills, hand–eye coordination skills, sequencing, following simple directions, labeling and describing, letter awareness, and color (primary and secondary) concepts. Optional: scissors skills.

Materials: You will need watercolor paper (or regular drawing paper), watercolor paints (or significantly diluted water-based paint), double-sided tape (or painter's tape), a brush, a cup, stencils of the children's initials, a fat marker or undiluted paint (one color), newspapers to cover the work surface, and scissors (optional).

Description: Draw the first name initial of the student (or any letter you are trying to teach) on a sheet of paper (approximately half the size of the paper being used for painting and about 2 inches (5 cm) wide) and cut it out. If appropriate, the child can help. Cover the work surface with newspapers.

Each student is given a sheet of watercolor/drawing paper. Using the tape, attach each letter to a separate sheet of drawing paper (if you are using painter's tape, tape the stencil around its perimeter). Encourage children to name each letter and the sound it makes ("Bill" starts with B and makes a "buh" sound).

Have the children pick the first color and start painting. Here is another opportunity to reinforce the letter: "blue" starts with B, the same letter as "Bill". There is no predetermined way to do it, but one of the good ways to create an interesting final project is to paint lines—horizontal, vertical, or diagonal (circles/wheels also create a nice effect). After the first line is done, ask the children to pick another color. A second line should be painted close to the first one, allowing the paint (and colors) to mix where both lines meet (a red line next to a yellow line will produce some orange color between them). Continue until the whole sheet of paper is painted.

While waiting for the paint to dry, ask children to help with the clean up. Carefully remove the stencil from the painting (a great activity for little fingers!). You should have a clear initial in the middle of the very colorful page.

Variations:

- Using a fat marker (or undiluted paint), outline the letter to make it stand out from the painting.

To make the stencil of the letter, use thick paper (i.e. cardstock) as it will protect the paper underneath from paint much better.

Always use extra caution when working with sharp tools such as scissors.

Straw Painting

Purpose: To develop visual attention to task, sequencing skills, hand–eye coordination, oral-motor skills, sequencing, following simple directions, labeling and describing, prepositions, and color (primary and secondary) concepts.

Materials: You will need newspaper to protect the work surface, removable (i.e. painter's) tape, plastic cups or other small containers for paint, drawing paper, poster paints, and plastic drinking straws.

Description: Ask students to cover the worktable with newspaper and tape one piece of drawing paper per student on top. If working with a group of students, designate a "helper" to complete those tasks. Allow students to choose the first color and place a large drop of paint on the drawing paper.

Instead of using brushes, ask students to use their straws to blow the paint around the paper.

Remember, this activity is not aimed at creating a painting of a house (which is possible, though), but is instead aimed at developing creativity, and it is about the process rather than the final product.

When it is not possible to blow the first color around anymore, provide students with the second color, in the same fashion as the first. Repeat this process as many times as necessary.

Allow students to choose their color and encourage them to use two colors of paint (i.e. Yellow and red), which will further enhance their knowledge of primary and secondary colors. The project is completed when the students are satisfied with the final outcome of their design.

Facilitate the clean-up process by designating one student to help, or by directing all the students to participate.

Variations:

- To make it a collaborative project, use one large piece of drawing paper instead of individual sheets.

- Using corn syrup (mixed with food coloring) instead of paint will create a shiny painting.

- Small-diameter straws will create intricate patterns, while large-diameter straws will create bolder designs.

If it is too difficult for students to blow the paint around, try diluting it with a little bit of water.

 Always use non-toxic paints. However, if you are concerned about students ingesting the paint, use corn syrup mixed with food coloring.

Recycled Bowling

Purpose: To develop hand–eye coordination, prehension (grasp), bilateral integration, visual-motor and scissors skills, motor planning, sequencing skills, math sense, measuring, ability to follow simple directions.

Materials: This activity requires ten paper-towel rolls, a ruler, markers/crayons/paints, glue, ribbon or yarn, white paper, scissors, a small ball (for the bowling game), and—optionally—stickers.

Description: Here is an activity that allows children to have fun with empty paper-towel rolls. Each student gets one paper-towel roll or, if you have fewer students in your group, distribute ten rolls evenly among students.

Ask the students to measure 3 inches (8 cm) from one end of each roll and make a mark with a marker or crayon. Using scissors, cut each roll across at the mark. Spread glue on each roll and wrap it in white paper, making sure one edge of the paper aligns with the edge of the roll.

Ask the children to tie the paper at the opposite end with a piece of ribbon or yarn, creating the look of a real bowling pin. Ask students to decorate their pins—there are no rules for this part. Foster their creativity by allowing them to use stickers, markers, crayons, or paints.

After all ten pins are finished, start a bowling game by setting all ten pins in a triangle (about 10 inches (25 cm) of space between them) and rolling the ball from 10 feet (3 m) away.

SPEAK, MOVE, PLAY AND LEARN WITH CHILDREN ON THE AUTISM SPECTRUM

Variations:

- Measuring is optional—you can ask children to mark the width of their hand on the roll.

- When working with a group of students, you can ask them to make all the pins with a common theme, i.e. sea/farm animals, favorite movie, etc.

- To create an activity promoting the acquisition of math skills, have children assign numbers to pins—during the game, children can identify numbers on pins, add them, compare scores, etc.

Some children will find it easier to decorate paper before gluing it to rolls.

Cutting paper rolls with scissors is much harder for little hands than cutting regular paper. You might need to provide additional assistance during this part of the project.

Tick-Tock

Purpose: To develop hand–eye coordination, grasp, scissor skills, sequencing skills, following simple directions, number sense, time concept, prepositions, and left/right concept.

Materials: You will need thick paper plates or ones made of Styrofoam or plastic, markers, poster board or heavy paper, paper fasteners (available at any stationery store), scissors, paper, and pencils.

Description: Let the children know they will be making their own clock. If you have an analog clock available, bring it as a model. Provide each child with a plate. Ask the children to mark a dot (or a small circle) at the top of each plate and one at the opposite side, using a marker or crayon. Ask students to write "12" just below the top mark and "6" slightly above the bottom dot.

Now ask the children to mark dots on each side, halfway in between the top and bottom. Students should write "9" next to the left dot and "3" next to the right dot. Use the analog clock as a model and ask students to fill in the missing numbers.

Using the poster board, have students draw and cut two arrows—a longer one for the minute hand, and a shorter one for the hour hand. Depending on the type of plates being used, use a sharpened pencil (for Styrofoam or paper plates) or the tip of scissors to make a small hole in the middle. Poke a hole in each hand and attach them to the "clock face" with the paper fastener, securing it in the back of the plate.

Variations:

- When teaching the time concept start with whole hours, then move to a half hour, a quarter hour and so on.

- Follow-up activity: create a written list of activities for a student or classroom. Now pick an activity and find its time on the clock. Or set the time on the clock and have the students identify the time and activity from the list.

Instead of making dots/circles, students can use various stickers—this is another way to further personalize their clocks.

 When using scissors to poke holes in plastic plates, place the plate on a stack of newspapers (or a flattened cardboard box), and apply gentle pressure to the scissors while rotating the plate. That way you will end up with a perfect hole, without risking an injury.

Cable Car

Purpose: This is a fun activity that facilitates gross motor movement and motor planning. It provides an opportunity for problem solving and working as a team. Small groups help build socialization and communication skills. It provides the opportunity to work on following multi-stepped directions. This activity also provides hands-on learning experience for concept building of heavy versus light.

Materials: To make the cable car you will need to cut the tops off two or three tissue boxes, depending on the number of children. Open two large paperclips so that there is a hook on both ends. Punch one end of the paperclip into the end of the tissue box. Do the same on the opposite end of the tissue box, ensuring the top hooks are positioned to be able to hang from a string. Gather a collection of objects, small enough to fit into the tissue box, commonly found around the classroom or household.

Description: Attach one end of a long piece of string to a wall with tape or thumbtack. Ensure it is at a height the children can get to safely. Attach the other end of the string to a desk or chair so that the string is at an angle when taut. Divide the children into small teams of two to four children. Assure the children that everyone will have a turn, then ask them to decide who will go first on their team.

Provide each team with a box of objects that they will use to send down the cable car. Give the teams instructions, such as, "Send eight items down the cable car." Encourage the children to discuss which objects would be heaviest. Ask the children to feel the objects, comparing and contrasting the weight of each one.

Once the team has decided on their objects, have the chosen team member place the items in the tissue box, and hang the box from the string. The team whose car reaches the end first wins. Continue to give the children various instructions with different requirements, such as, "Add seven items to the cable car; two of them must be red" or "Add five items; one item must be the lightest in your box." Discuss the concept of heavy versus light.

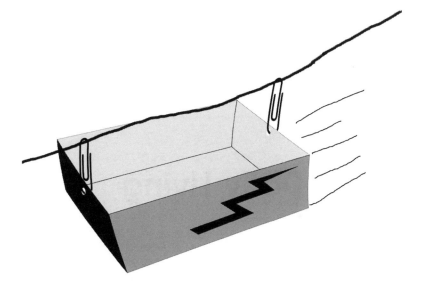

Variations:

- For younger or cognitively impaired children, simplify the instructions, such as, "Place the largest item in the car" or "Place a yellow item in your car." This provides the opportunity to discuss basic concepts of colors, shapes, and large versus small.

CHAPTER 8

Activities of Daily Living

Activities of daily living consist of anything we do to maintain our bodies and living space. This can be as simple as brushing hair or trimming fingernails up to managing bank accounts and bills. The latter are commonly referred to as "instrumental activities of daily living."

In working with children identified with mental and emotional challenges, one of the major concerns we hear consistently from parents is their frustration around getting their child ready and out the door in the morning. Many parents express their concerns about their children's lack of independence in this area. Parents and teachers are often busy with limits on their time; therefore, they develop convenient strategies to save time and frustration, which typically means doing it for the child. This does not allow the child to gain these skills through developing a plan and a sense of routine.

This chapter will help children to refine skills such as grooming, cleaning, and dressing in a fun, non-threatening manner that allows them to integrate these tasks into their routine. It is best to introduce these activities in a playful, joyous manner at a time when there is no rush. Encourage children to discuss what it is they are doing, and how it is important and helpful in their daily lives. For example, "I brush my teeth to keep my mouth clean so I do not get cavities. It is also important when I am speaking to others that my breath is not stinky." This helps children internalize the importance of the activities and understand that they are done not only for themselves, but also to be socially appropriate and acceptable to others.

Provide enough support for children to complete the task successfully. However, encourage them next time to do a little more on their own. You may provide a picture sequence of each step (for example, teeth brushing or shoe tying) in the area where they will be engaging in the task. This provides visual support so that the child does not have to count on an adult to verbalize each and every step in the sequence.

Hair Flair

Purpose: To work on comparing and contrasting, brushing hair, fine/gross motor movements, body awareness, crossing midline, upper quadrant range of motion, sensory integration, attributes, and expressive vocabulary through labeling.

Materials: You will need a brush or comb and a mirror.

For the variations you might need bows, bobby pins, hair clips, scrunchies, headbands, hair products, and shaving cream.

Description: Have the students pick out a brush and hold it in their hands. Label what color the brush is, talk about how the handle is smooth and the bristles are rough, and describe the color and whether the brush is hard or soft.

Have them practice brushing their hair and, as they are doing so, count the strokes so they can practice saying numbers. Then have the students practice putting on bows, hair clips, bobby pins, scrunchies, headbands, hair products, and so on. Label all the hair accessories and products and describe how they feel (gel feels cold and wet). Finally, have the children say how they feel now that their hair is done (I feel pretty, clean, sleek, silky, etc.). See the Appendix for a list of descriptors.

Variations:

- For some students you can use an adaptive hair brush or a vibrating hair brush, which will make them more likely to want to hold on to the brush or play with it.

- Use shaving cream on boys' hair and have them comb it out with a comb. They can draw lines in their hair with the comb and get excited when the shaving cream disappears while they are combing. Their hair will smell nice so you can talk about the scent as well.

- Go to a second-hand store and buy lots of different wigs. Have the students compare and contrast the differences in the wigs and hair types—for example, long, medium and short hair; blonde, red, brunette, gray; curly, straight, wavy, spiky; multicolored clown; coarse, thin, smooth; and so forth. Then have the students practice brushing the hair on the wigs.

- If wigs are out of your budget then getting Barbies™ at garage sales or at discount stores can help keep costs down and also add tools that the students love to use.

On Your Marks, Get Set, Get Dressed!

Purpose: To increase the ability to perform activities of daily living, dexterity, labeling and describing clothing, teamwork, and bilateral integration. Practicing this activity may even help children get dressed quicker in the morning and avoid the frustration that comes with a time crunch.

Materials: You will need various pieces of large-size clothing with buttons, zippers, snaps and ties. Clothing should be large enough to fit over the students' everyday attire.

Description: Students sit in a circle and label or describe all the articles of clothing to be used. They can practice snaps, buttons and zippers at this time. After they have labeled, described and practiced with the fasteners, place all clothing in a pile at one end of the room.

Students line up at the opposite end of the room behind a "starting line." When the teacher says, "Ready—get set—get dressed," the students race to the pile of clothing, put it on and race back to the finish line. When they catch their breath, they can tell you what they are wearing. Parents love this activity as it helps getting children dressed in a hurry in the morning.

Please resist the urge to help with buttons, snaps, zippers, and fasteners.

Variations:

- Have students pair up and dress each other.
- Use this activity with shoes and socks only. They can use their own shoes and socks.
- After students are finished they can sort, fold and put the clothing away.

Shoes and Socks

Purpose: This lesson supports the activities of daily living and increases the use of descriptors, in-hand awareness, constructional praxis, and body awareness.

Materials: You will need shoes and socks, Bubble Wrap®, ice cubes, a spray bottle, a feather, sandpaper, and anything that has texture, vibration, or is a different temperature. See the Appendix for help with descriptors.

Description: Have students sit in a circle. They should be instructed to take off their shoes and socks. They can then walk around, feeling the floor with their feet and describing the surface they are walking on. If Bubble Wrap is available, let students pop bubbles with their feet. They can use their imaginations to complete the carrier phrase, "This feels like——."

Students should return to the circle and sit with their legs and feet stretched toward the middle of the circle. The teacher should then use different objects or materials to rub on the bottom and sides of their feet. Students should describe each texture and how it feels. This activity is a lot of fun and gets many giggles.

Variations:

- While students are sitting in a circle with feet stretched toward the middle of the circle, they should close their eyes while the teacher rubs materials and objects on their feet. Students need to guess what the teacher has rubbed on their feet.

- While students are sitting with feet in the middle, the teacher can squeeze their toes, ankles and feet while labeling each. The students usually enjoy this activity and request more. The teacher should ask students to label the part of the foot to be squeezed, ("Squeeze my toe, please"). The teacher may wear gloves to protect their hands.

- After students take off their shoes and socks, mix them up and have them request from each other their own shoes and socks without pointing.

Sock Ball Pitch

Purpose: To develop describing, giving attributes, vocabulary building, in-hand manipulation, dexterity, bilateral integration, aim, sensory integration, and expressive vocabulary.

Materials: The activity requires socks of different shapes, colors, sizes, textures, and kinds (e.g. Toe-socks).

Description: Take a basketful of socks of all kinds and have the student empty the contents onto a table or a bed. Help the child pick pairs of socks and take turns describing how the socks feel, look, and smell (from fabric detergent). Try to have them describe as much as possible and, if the student runs out of things to say, teach him or her some new words. See the Appendix for help with descriptors.

Once the students have described the texture and color and found the right pair, have them roll the socks into little sock-balls. Once the ball is done the student gets to throw the sock-ball into the basket or a drawer as his reward.

Variations:

- The number of variables for the socks should match the functioning level of the student. Add more colors, shapes, sizes, and textures for higher functioning students or as the student progresses toward their goal.

- Most schools have laundry rooms to teach activities of daily living so you can even start the project when you are washing the socks. Have the students throw the socks into the washer every time they label or give a description of the sock. After the socks are dry, have the student take them from the dryer and express how warm the socks feel.

- You can take pictures of kids wearing different pairs of socks and then have them match the sock-ball with the picture for a different twist.

Make Your Bed

Purpose: This is a perfect activity to help students learn how to manage large sheets, blankets, and folding, and ultimately make their own beds. "Make Your Bed" also supports teamwork, motor coordination, labeling, giving and taking directions, and using adverbs.

Materials: A large sheet or blanket and a pillow are all that is needed for this activity. If there are more than four participants then use two sheets or blankets and two pillows.

Description: Have a student carefully unfold the sheet or blanket. Each student should have a turn at grasping the sheet at two corners, shaking it, pulling it up in the air, and letting it slowly fall down as if making a bed. Depending on the number of participants, each can grasp one or two corners of the sheet. Start by having all participants shake the sheet and make waves or pull the sheet above their heads and down to the floor to make it look like a parachute, mushroom or bubble.

Next, have the students take turns giving directions to each other. For example, "Everyone move to the right," "Hold the sheet above your head," "Shake slow," "Shake fast," "Shake it behind your back," and so on.

Add a pillow on the sheet and work as a team to move the pillow from side to side or bounce it up and down. Choose a student to give the pillow to and use teamwork to move the pillow toward that person. Have one student give directions on how to move the pillow toward another student or in a particular fashion. Last, students can fold the sheet or blanket and put it away.

Variations:

- For faster action, use a ball or stuffed animal instead of a pillow.

- Increase the difficulty by moving forward, backward, circling left or right while moving the pillow around on the blanket.

- You can use a long desk or put many desks together to form a "bed" in school for practicing purposes.

Clean Your Room Too

Purpose: This is a highly motivating way to teach the skills of matching, sorting, folding, cleaning up, describing and counting.

Materials: This activity requires 10–15 pairs of socks, and painter's tape or chalk to mark the midline.

Description: Students can use masking tape or chalk to mark the midline of the room or outdoor area. Divide students and adults into two teams. Each team begins with an equal number of socks on opposing sides of the midline. On the first signal, the players toss the socks over the midline to the opposing team as fast as possible.

On the second signal, the players stop tossing, and the instructor announces, "Clean your room." Players then collect all the socks on their side of the midline and count them. The team with fewer socks is the winner. Now you can play again or sort, match, fold, and put away. Players can take turns asking for a matching sock. For example, "Does anyone have a brown sock with yellow stripes?"

Variations:

- Try different types of soft clothing or household items, such as dish towels, wash rags, T-shirts or underclothes. Mix them up well—just remember to sort, describe, fold, and put them away at the end of the game.

- Students can describe what the room looks like before and after the game—for example, a mess, a disaster, or "a hurricane hit this place."

- Use music to signal the beginning of the game and stop the music to signal the end of the game.

- To add a challenge, teams can play the game with their backs to the midline and the opposing players.

ACTIVITIES OF DAILY LIVING

135

Hidden Messages

Purpose: This activity helps develop handwriting skills. It encourages improved bilateral integration and visual-motor skills. It is geared toward improving social skills by encouraging children to share personal information and interests. It provides opportunities for peers to engage in conversation and ask questions about each other.

Materials: For this activity you will need a white tapered candle and a piece of white, unlined paper. You will later need watercolor paints and paintbrushes.

Description: Lay down a generous amount of newspaper at a large group table. Call on the child who is exhibiting the most appropriate behavior and ask them to pass out the materials. Comment on the desired behavior—for example, "I like the way Sally's hands are sitting nicely in her lap and her body is turned toward me."

Once the candles and paper are distributed, ask the children to write the answers to a series of questions on the paper, using the candle like a pencil. Encourage the children to press down hard enough so that the wax sticks to the paper, while pointing out that you cannot see the words on the page. Encourage them to keep their answers to themselves. Determine the best questions to ask, depending on the group's age, cognitive level, and known shared interest.

These are a few sample subjects for questions: favorite superhero, favorite movie, color hair/eyes, favorite sport/sports team, number of brothers/sisters, or family pets.

Collect the papers from each student, and mix them so that they are in random order. Redistribute the papers to the group members along with the watercolor paints and paintbrushes. Have the children color the paper with watercolors, encouraging them to use friendly requests when sharing materials. Look for the answers written in wax. Discuss why you can see the words, and how the wax interacted with the watercolor paints.

Have each child read the answers on their page and ask the group to think about whom they think wrote those answers. Encourage the group to use critical thinking and problem solving amongst each other to determine who the individual is. For example, "This person's favorite superhero is Spiderman, and we know Max has a Spiderman lunchbox."

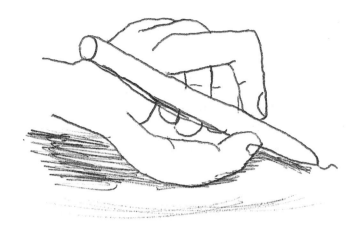

Variations:

- To use this activity with younger children or cognitively impaired children have them write down their initials and have the group determine who the individual is by their initials.

 For younger children with a less developed grasp, break a candle into smaller pieces so that it fits in the palm of their hands.

Animal House

Purpose: This activity teaches children the value of the final stage of play: cleaning up. It allows children to take responsibility for their environment, and ownership of their toys and games. The activity provides increased proprioceptive input with gross motor movements focusing on bilateral coordination of the right and left side of the body. It allows children to produce novel animal sounds and practice various sound patterns.

Materials: You will need a pillowcase. Depending on the number of items you expect to be cleaned up, it can be large or small. Prior to introducing this activity have a pillowcase (or multiple pillowcases) prepared with a ribbon, sewn or safety-pinned to opposite sides of the opened end of the pillowcase so that it can tie around the child's waist or chest.

Description: This activity is best introduced at the end-of-the-day clean-up, in the house or classroom. Have the children pick an animal they would like to imitate. Suggestions include kangaroo, bunny, turtle, frog, birds, and many others.

Ask the children to make the sounds the animal they have chosen makes while they move around the room like that animal. Encourage the children to pick up their toys, games, and clothes and put them in their pouch as they scramble around the room making animal noises. For animals where the child would be on all fours, have the children put the pillowcase on their back and encourage them to balance the contents on their back.

Variations:

- Divide the toys up by color, theme, or letters in their names, and make it a scavenger hunt.

Brushy, Brushy, Brushy

Purpose: This activity teaches children how to brush their teeth. The children create a model of their mouth, so they can easily visualize brushing the portions of the mouth not easily reached. The activity provides opportunities to practice fine motor control, and facilitates a pincer grasp.

Materials: For this activity you will need play-dough, colorful square-shaped gum, and a toothbrush.

Description: Choose a child representing good behavior to pick his or her play-dough color. Have the children make two quarter-inch thick (5 mm), oval shapes with the play-dough by pressing down with the palm of their hand to flatten them. Ask them to count out the number of pieces of gum they will use for the top and bottom. Covering half of the play-dough shape, push the square pieces of gum along the edge, aligning them to represent teeth. Do this for the second piece of play-dough.

Place the two pieces of play-dough on top of each other so that the gum is in the middle for both pieces. Using the toothbrush, have the children practice brushing all sides of the square gum, discussing getting to the back pieces. Have them lift the upper piece and brush the inside of the gum squares. Encourage them to use gentle pressure so that the gum pieces do not move, as this is the right amount of pressure to use with brushing their actual teeth. Discuss oral hygiene and the importance of brushing teeth.

Variations:

- Instead of gum squares use coins.

- For older children, discuss the different types of teeth and organize them by gum color.

- For younger children, use the same color gum—for example, blue—to represent the back teeth on both sides, upper and lower. During actual brushing in the morning or evening you can remind the child to make sure to clean their "blue" teeth.

139

Necktie It Up!

Purpose: This activity helps develop fine motor skills and bilateral integration. It also helps children learn and practice the steps of shoe tying.

Materials: For this activity you will need two neckties from Dad or Grandpa's closet (be sure to get permission) and a piece of cardboard or poster board 2 foot (50 cm) by 2 foot. In the cardboard, cut out two rows of three holes, making sure the holes are in alignment to the hole on the opposite side. In preparation, tie the two thick ends of the ties together so that it is one long piece, with the skinny part of the tie at either end.

Description: Have the children discuss the ties they brought in, focusing on the colors, patterns, or a story of when their family member wore it.

Place the pre-made knot under the cardboard between the top circles and pull both ends of the neckties through the holes. Demonstrate lacing the neckties through the holes to represent lacing a shoe.

Once at the end of the holes, teach the children the seven steps of shoe-tying, having them verbalize each step while completing it to help integrate the steps into their long-term memory. The seven steps of shoe tying are:

1. Cross laces.

2. Put through.

3. Pull tight.

4. Make loops.

5. Cross loops.

6. Put through.

7. Pull tight.

Variations:

- Decorate a Father's Day gift using the necktie bows.

"Go Fish" for Socks

Purpose: This is a super creative way to encourage students to communicate, sort, describe, fold, and match.

Materials: All you need for this activity is approximately five pairs of socks and a container for each participant. An additional container or bag is needed to represent the "fishpond." Separate the socks from their pairs and mix them up.

Description: "Go Fish" has been a favorite card came for decades. This variation replaces the cards with socks in order to build skills in communication and daily living.

Begin by having students sit in a circle on the floor or at a table. Pass out five socks into each player's bag and place the remaining socks into the "fishpond." Determine who goes first by picking a number, drawing straws, or whatever method works best for your group.

The first player looks into their container, picks a sock and asks another student, "Do you have a sock that is ——?" If player 2 has the sock, he or she must hand it to the first player. If player 2 does not have the sock then he or she says, "Go Fish."

Player 1 then fishes a sock out of the "fishpond" and adds it to his or her container. When a player makes a match, he or she should fold or roll the socks. The player with the most rolls/pairs after all the socks have been matched is the winner.

Match the socks to the ability level of the students: plain socks for beginners and colorful, striped, knee socks, anklets, etc. for more experienced players.

Review the socks prior to playing the game. For example, "This is a light-blue girl's sock with hearts on the top" or "This is a plain-white men's sweat sock." This will give the students an idea of how detailed their descriptions should be. See the Appendix for help with descriptors.

Variations:

- This game can be played with gloves and mittens or mixed gloves, mittens and socks.

- For beginners, or players who may need a bit more practice, do not use containers, or use see-through plastic bags. Simply lay the socks out in front of each player. Continue using the "fishpond" container.

ACTIVITIES OF DAILY LIVING

Pet Care Practice

Purpose: The students will learn independent activities of daily living (ADLs), foster a sense of responsibility and independence, explore human bonds with animals, learn a trade for vocational reasons, practice sequencing of multi-step projects, learn to follow directions, label, describe, and manipulate a can opener.

Materials: For this activity you will need two bowls, canned dog food, a can opener, and a spoon or fork.

Description: The best thing students can do is to learn how to take care of themselves. And once they have accomplished this they can then take care of their pets. You can start this activity by having the students label all the materials. Once they have labeled them, ask them what each item is used for. If they give you an answer, give them an opportunity to touch the item and describe some of its attributes. For instance, a fork is hard, made of metal, sharp at the points, and has four prongs. A bowl is round, deep, hard, and made of plastic or glass.

Now that the labeling and describing has been done, give each student an opportunity to open the can of dog food with the can opener. Give them multi-stepped directions and make sure they are following these correctly. Add prompts and models if they need them.

Once they have opened the can of dog food, instruct them to pour the contents into the bowl carefully. They must try to be as neat as possible. Practice makes perfect so, needless to say, the first few tries will be a bit messy.

Have them use the forks or spoons to scoop out all the contents. Then the students can place the dog food bowls on the floor and call their pets.

If this is being done at school you can have another student pretend to be the dog, and this will allow one student to practice calling their pet and another student to follow directions and come when called.

When you are using can openers please make sure to choose the ones that do not leave a sharp edge. There are openers on the market that leave a soft and blunt edge after cutting.

Variations:

- For students who are more advanced, you can have them mix in dry food with the wet can food. This will help them learn to mix ingredients without spilling.

- Once the students have mastered opening cans, give them pull-tab cans to practice this kind of can opening.

Recycling Round-Up

Purpose: In this activity the students will learn the symbol for things that can be recycled, and how to sort, follow multi-step directions, ask Wh-questions, and use their balance and proprioception to gather and crush the cans.

Materials: You will need plastic bags, non-latex gloves (if there are allergies to latex), and a picture of the symbol for items that can be recycled.

Description: Begin the activity by printing out a picture of the symbol for your country for items that can be recycled. Show the picture to the children and have them see that the arrows stand for "reduce, re-use and recycle." You might want to give them a little lesson on how much garbage humans produce per year and how we can help our environment by recycling items.

Next, explain to them how you will be setting up a recycling program in your class. Have them designate three bins, cans, or boxes for this purpose. Label the receptacles "Glass," "Plastic," and "Aluminum," and ask the students to remember to put their cans, bottles or aluminum foil in these once they are empty.

Have the students go around the room after breakfast, lunch, and snacks to request the bottles or cans from other students. Have them use full sentences and make sure that they use good manners. The students chosen to go around the room collecting the bottles should have a plastic bag so that they don't have to carry the big receptacle. One student should carry a bag for glass bottles, another for cans, and yet another for plastic bottles.

Once they are done gathering the items they can pour out the bag into the appropriate receptacle. This can be tricky, but please let the students do this without your help. It will teach them valuable daily living skills. If they spill they can just pick up all the items off the floor and sort them into the correct receptacles. Make sure the students are wearing their gloves when sorting.

If there is broken glass, have the teacher do the clean up to prevent any accidents.

You can drop a bunch of aluminum cans on the floor and have the students step on them to crush them. This will create more room for more recycling in your bin, but will also help the students balance on one foot while crushing with the other.

Variations:

- Involve other classrooms, and have your class make recycle bins for them to put in their classes. Then have your kids go once a week and request the bins so you can have the recyclables.

- Take some students to the recycling center so they can get money for their items.

- Plan a party with the money made from recycling. Point out that the environment wins and so does the class.

- Have the students guess how much money they will get back from the recycling. The one who is closest to the real amount gets to decide what to do with the money (picnic, movies, pizza party).

- For higher functioning or life skills classes have the students make a graph of which items made more money. Have them compare and contrast the glass, plastic, and aluminum.

The Gift of Giving

Purpose: To learn to follow multi-step directions, folding, manipulating with fine motor and gross motor movements, labeling, and describing.

Materials: You will need boxes, wrapping paper, tape, and ribbons.

Description: Explain to the kids about how important it is to know how to wrap presents. Throughout our lives we have many occasions when we have the opportunity to give gifts to others, and we need to learn how to make those gifts look beautiful.

Ask the kids to tell you the name of an occasion when a gift is a nice thing to give. Examples can include, but are not limited to, birthdays, anniversaries, weddings, Valentine's Day, Mother's Day, Father's Day, Easter, and Christmas.

Now show the kids the boxes you have and have them ask for the box they want by describing it. They should use as many descriptors as possible. For example, they can say, "I want the rectangular, flat, little blue box please."

After choosing their box they will have to ask for their wrapping paper in the same way: "I want the red wrapping paper with the blue flowers please."

Once everyone has a piece of paper and a box, the teacher then begins to give directions on how to wrap the box. The teacher can explain the process as fast or as slowly as the group needs. When they are done, the kids can keep the box for themselves as a nice little decoration or give it to someone as a joke gift, since the box is empty.

Variations:

- Go to the dollar store and give each student a dollar so they can buy a buddy a present. Then have them wrap the present for their friend once they get back to school.

- Have "Bucket Buddies" where each week they have to wrap something up for a friend and put it in their friend's bucket. Trade friends every month to make new friends.

- For a more challenging activity have the students learn to tie ribbons around the boxes.

CHAPTER 9

The Miracle of Music

We call this chapter "The Miracle of Music" because we have seen how music can enrich, motivate, and influence students beyond belief, like a miracle. Whipple (2004) conducted a meta-analysis of music therapies that were used with students on the spectrum. She concluded that "all music intervention, regardless of purpose or implementation, has been effective for children and adolescents with autism."

Utilizing the energy of music, rhythm, and movement can be a significant factor in meeting many therapeutic goals relating to:

- verbal and non-verbal communication

- fine and gross motor skills

- auditory processing and listening skills

- shared attention

- social pragmatic skills of group interactions, topic maintenance, and turn taking.

In addition to using music to meet goals, we have provided ideas on how to build and use your own simple musical instruments. Students will reap the added benefits of pride, creativity, problem solving, and teamwork from the experience of creating a unique instrument before using it to interact with others. Once your students have created their avant-garde musical instruments, let the music and movement begin.

Below are some of our favorite activities that have inspired students to move, stomp, march, sing, and communicate.

- Have a Jam session—challenge all students to play to the beat of a favorite song, or sing a song and accompany it with their instruments.

- Create an impromptu parade, drum circle, or band to entertain family, friends, and teachers.

- Assign a conductor for your newly formed band or orchestra. Students can take turns directing others to keep the beat, slow down, speed up, raise and lower volume, etc.

- Get students to listen to a rhythm and then duplicate it with their instruments. Alternatively, students can listen to an instrument and attempt to imitate the musical sounds with their voices.

- When no instruments are available, have students create music with their bodies by clapping, snapping, stomping, humming, whistling, and tapping.

- Creating sound effects—such as the wind, footsteps, a door closing, crickets chirping, etc.—to accompany a story is a great way to encourage listening and doing.

- Have students perform a solo act or introduce a fellow student's solo act as a wonderful way to encourage communication and build self-esteem.

So grab your empty boxes, elastic bands, straws, and paper plates and start making music!

The Tambourine

Purpose: The purpose of this activity is to promote fine motor skills, listening skills, symbolic play, imagination, requesting, and hand–eye coordination.

Materials: You will need two paper plates per student, crayons or markers, dried beans, streamers (different colors, long and short), tape, and a stapler.

Description: The instructor should have the crayons and markers. Students will request crayons or markers by color to decorate the bottom sides of their paper plates. After the students have decorated their paper plates, have each student talk about and describe what they drew.

Put one paper plate on the table with the right side up. Students will request (by color and length) tape streamers to add to the bottom half of the plate. Place the second plate on top of the first one, right side down.

Staple the edges together, letting students ask for help if needed, and making sure to leave an opening at the top for a handful of dried beans. Pour in the beans and then staple the opening shut. You are now ready to play your tambourine.

Variations:

- Have students tap out rhythms against different parts of their bodies (e.g. leg, foot, arm, tummy).

- Have students listen to a rhythm and duplicate it on the tambourine.

- Have students shake the tambourine behind their backs, under the leg, above their heads, with the right hand, with the left hand, upside down, with their eyes closed, fast, slow, etc.

The Flute

Purpose: To promote breath control, lung capacity, fine motor skills, cutting, bilateral coordination, in-hand manipulation, dexterity, listening skills, and creativity.

Materials: You will need paper-towel or toilet-paper rolls, wax paper, rubber bands, and pencils, crayons, and markers.

Description: The student uses the pencil to poke three or four holes in the cardboard roll, about 1 inch (2.5 cm) apart. Count each hole as you make it and, after all are complete, decorate the tube with crayons or markers. Have the student cut a 4 inch (10 cm) square of wax paper. Secure the wax paper over one end of the cardboard roll using the rubber band. If the student needs assistance, let him or her ask for help. You are now ready to play!

Variations:

- Have the students duplicate sound patterns made by the instructor.
- Have students hum a favorite song and the others guess what song it is.
- Pretend you are in a parade or marching band.

The Drum

Purpose: To promote bilateral coordination, listening skills, fine motor strength and coordination, symbolic play, and creativity.

Materials: For this activity you will need cans with lids or oatmeal boxes, colored paper, glue or tape, brown paper bags, rubber bands, and crayons and markers.

Description: Have each student choose their favorite color. Cut the paper so that it fits around the can. Use crayons and markers to decorate and sign the paper (the adult should have the crayons and markers and students should request colors). Each student shows and talks about their decorated paper.

Tape the paper onto the can. Cut a circle from the paper bag (approximately 4 inches (10 cm) larger in diameter than the can opening). Students can then crumple the paper in their hands so it looks like leather. The instructor can talk about crumpling, crunching, and squeezing with one hand and both hands.

With the lid on the can, place a few drops of glue on the lid. Flatten out your circle and center it over the lid. Have students place a rubber band over the lid to hold the paper bag securely on the can. Students are now ready to tap out rhythms.

Variations:

• Have students sit in a drum circle and keep rhythm with each other.

• Students can listen to a pattern and duplicate the pattern.

• Students can tap their feet to the rhythm of the drum and their favorite songs.

The Box Guitar

Purpose: Besides making a cool guitar to rock out, your students will learn shape identification, bilateral coordination, creativity, bilateral integration, describing, requesting, and sequencing skills.

Materials: The only items truly required for a box guitar are a box and an assortment of elastic bands of various thicknesses. Decorations are optional but could include wrapping paper, paint, stickers, markers, and/or crayons.

Description: Depending on the setting, students can search their environment for a box or request a box from the instructor. Once a box has been found or requested, students can choose a shape to be carved into the front of the box.

First, have the students draw an outline of the shape on the middle of the box. Next, each student should cut the shape from the front of the box.

Resist the urge to cut the shape or wrap the elastic bands for the students. Let the students struggle to cut the shape out of the box, even if it is too small or too large. Only help if the student requests help.

Once the shape is cut out of the box, students can decorate, cover or color their box.

Last, students can ask for up to five elastic bands of various thicknesses to stretch around their box until the bands are fairly taut. Discuss, demonstrate, and have students discover that the thick bands make a low tone and the thin bands make a high tone. Give students the option to swap elastic bands to make their guitar have a distinct sound. Now have a jam session to a favorite song.

Variations:

- Students can glue or tape on a ruler, stick, or paper-towel roll for the guitar neck.

- Some students may want string or yarn so that the guitar can be worn around the neck.

If you use string, make sure it can be easily broken or will break away from the guitar to reduce the risk of choking.

- Have a foot guitar jam and play with your toes. Students don't expect this and it's worth a ton of giggles.

- The box guitar can double as a percussion instrument. Strum-strum-tap-tap.

The Ghungroos

Purpose: A ghungroo is a musical anklet with many bells strung together and is worn by classical Indian dancers. While making and wearing ghungroos, students will learn descriptors, auditory processing, patterning, motor planning, bilateral integration, and hand–eye coordination.

Materials: To make ghungroos you will need to gather a selection of beads and bells. Beads should have a hole large enough to accommodate a pipe cleaner, sturdy elastic band, shoelace, or strand of leather.

Using a sturdy elastic band will make it easy to put on or remove the Ghungroo.

This is not a good activity if your child is at risk of putting the beads or bells into his or her mouth.

Description: Ghungroos are very easy to make, yet so motivating and fun that we make them as reinforcers for the students completing their academic tasks. Simply string the beads and bells onto the pipe cleaner or strand of choice and have the students tie this around their ankles.

Of course, students have to request the color and size of the beads and bells and choose the type of fastener they want. Also, students are encouraged to use and verbalize patterns—for example, bead-bead-bead-bell. Patterns can also be established by the teacher and presented to the students auditorily, visually, or both. Once all students have fastened their ghungroos onto their ankles, they can dance, jump, stomp, and shake their feet in the air.

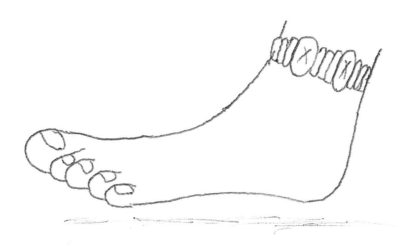

Variations:

- Students can take turns establishing a bell pattern by stomping, tapping, or shaking their feet, and the other students attempt to copy the pattern.

- Ghungroos can also be made for the wrists for twice as much jingle fun.

- Make and add more ghungroos so that as students grow and become more advanced in their footwork they can perform for an audience.

The Oboe Straw

Purpose: Wind instruments are an excellent way to increase oral motor strength and coordination. Fine motor movements and sequencing will also be strengthened with this activity.

Materials: For this activity you will need a variety of non-bendable plastic straws and scissors.

Description: Place a variety of straws in front of the students and have each student request the straw they want for this activity. Begin by flattening about half an inch (1 cm) on one end of the straw by pinching it between your finger and thumb.

Next, use the scissors to cut a point on the flattened end of the straw.

At this point the student can blow through the pointed end of the straw to get a monotone sound. Last, cut or poke two small quarter-inch (5 mm) holes about a third and a quarter of the way down the straw from the point. Now the student can make different tones by closing up the holes one at a time or both at the same time.

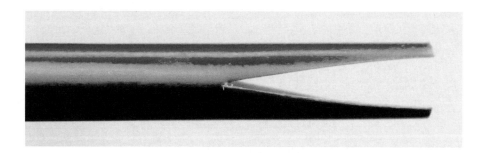

Variations:

- Experiment with different sizes or lengths of straws and talk about the different tones each makes.

- Start a marching band and march around the classroom, halls, or kitchen.

- Add structure by playing to the beat of a song such as "Twinkle, Twinkle Little Star" or "Old MacDonald Had a Farm."

- Cut four oboe straws into lengths, approximately 8, 7, 6, and 5 inches (20, 17, 15, and 12 cm) long. Place a three-inch (7 cm) piece of masking or duct tape on a table, sticky side up. Place the straws "reed" side up, about one inch (2.5 cm) below the tape line, arranging them from longest to shortest. Leave about half an inch (1 cm) between the straws.

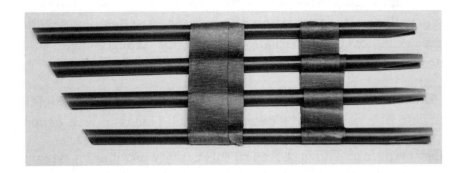

• Or place the straws directly next to one another.

• Place a second piece of tape over the straws and seal onto the first piece of tape. Seal tape between straws for a homemade pan flute.

Pan flutes are an ancient musical instrument named after the Greek god Pan who would play this instrument.

Be careful with the cut ends of the straws as they may have sharp points—use scissors to round off any sharp points prior to playing the instrument.

157

The Castanets

Purpose: Castanets are traditionally used with lively music and storytelling. This adaptation of a castanet will help your students master the skills of finger isolation, dexterity, storytelling, sequencing and describing.

Materials: To make castanets you will need four small, metal bottle caps or lids, one pair of old gloves, four small pieces of wax paper, and glue.

Description: The first step to this activity is obtaining permission to use an old pair of gloves. Making castanets gives the instructor a functional opportunity to talk about and label the fingers. Students can practice wiggling fingers in isolation, in pairs, or by making gestural hand shapes.

To make the castanets put a few drops of glue inside each bottle cap. Crumple the wax paper and stuff it into the thumb and index finger of the glove, then press the front of the thumb and index finger into the glue, and let it dry. While the glue is drying pass around a piece of wax paper and have the students describe it both before and after it is crumpled.

The instructor can also use this time to talk about how castanets are used to enhance storytelling by providing sound effects. After the glue has dried, remove the wax paper and slide your hand into the glove to begin creating music and making sound effects. As a group, practice making sounds for rain, walking, running, frying, sizzling, etc. Give each student an opportunity to tell a story or create music with their castanets.

Variations:

- Glue castanets of various sizes on all the fingers of the glove to build more finger dexterity and sound-variation skills.

- For a change, glue or sew bells onto the finger of the gloves. Students may want a combination of bottle caps and bells to create original music.

- Accompany the fingers with the toes by gluing bottle caps on the bottom of the toes and bells on the top.

Do not attempt to walk or run with bottle caps on the bottom of your feet. They are for musical purposes only and should only be tapped on the floor.

158

The Me Band

Purpose: Using your own body to create sounds, rhythms, and music promotes muscle coordination, muscle isolation, bilateral integration, oral motor coordination, auditory processing, sensory integration, body-part awareness, and identification.

Materials: For this activity you need nothing except yourselves.

Description: This is the best, most creative, anytime, anywhere activity ever. Start at your head and work down to your toes, experimenting with and discussing the sounds your body can make:

- mouth: whistling, clicking, clucking, popping, trilling, hissing, etc.
- hands: snapping, clapping, patting, drumming, rubbing, etc.
- feet: stomping, stamping, tap dancing, etc.
- toes: tapping.

Students can practice making sounds to different tempos at various volumes, and making more than one sound at a time. Now put them all together to the beat of a lively song.

Variations:

- The instructor or a student stands or sits behind the group so he or she cannot be seen, and produces a sound with a beat. Students need to guess how the sound was made and reproduce the beat.
- Songs can be choreographed so that all students stomp, clap, or snap at certain points in the song. Choreography can be simple or complex to fit the ability level of the students.
- Students can take turns calling out sounds and a number of repetitions—for example, stomp twice, clap once, whistle a tune, and tap to the back wall.

159

Tap, Rub, Pinch, Shake

Purpose: Making this four-in-one musical instrument builds skills in the areas of describing, using verbs, sequencing, fine and gross motor strength, and coordination.

Materials: You will need one or two clean, empty tin cans (ribbed on the side) for each student, colorful balloons, elastic bands, various grains, pebbles or beans, and sticks or chopsticks.

Description:

Use can openers that do not leave sharp edges.

Begin by having each student choose their can(s), their balloon (by color) and type of grain, bean, or both. Students can then add a handful of the desired grain/beans into the can.

Next, each student will simply cut the end off the balloon and stretch it over the open end of their can(s). To ensure that all the balloons stay in place, secure them with elastic bands and *voilà*, you have a four-in-one musical instrument!

All students can now have fun shaking, tapping, rubbing the sides of the can with a stick, and pinching the top of the balloons to make a thumping sound. Each student can describe their instrument, how they made it, what their favorite sound is, and how to make different sounds. Last, have a parade or dance circle along with motivating music.

SPEAK, MOVE, PLAY AND LEARN WITH CHILDREN ON THE AUTISM SPECTRUM

Variations:

- Students can attempt to tap instruments with their toes and shake them with their feet.

- Experiment with different types and quantities of objects to put inside the cans and discuss the changes in sound.

- Play a guessing game by having students identify what and how many objects are in the can by just listening.

- Replace tin cans with rigid plastic bottles that have screw caps.

Use duct tape or electrical tape instead of, or in addition to, elastic bands as this will help the balloons to stay on better.

The Harmonica

Purpose: This activity promotes fine motor development and bilateral integration. It provides oral motor input and promotes regular and sustained breathing. It improves auditory processing and speed.

Materials: To make the harmonica you will need two tongue depressors, tape, scissors, paper, and three wide rubber bands (such as those used to hold vegetables).

Description: Trace the outline of the two tongue depressors on a piece of paper. Cut out the tongue depressor shapes so that you have two, long, rectangular pieces of paper. Stack two tongue depressors on top of one another and wrap the long, rectangular pieces of paper around the width of the tongue depressors. Secure the paper loops with a piece of tape so that they stay in a circular shape.

Remove the paper loops. Separate the tongue depressors and slide both loops onto one tongue depressor. Stretch a rubber band lengthwise over the tongue depressor and two paper loops. Stack the second tongue depressor under the first and secure the two tongue depressors by wrapping rubber bands around each end.

To play the harmonica blow between the tongue depressors while sliding the paper loops to change the pitch.

Allow the children to explore the harmonica and the sounds it creates to familiarize themselves with various tones and pitches. Have the children sit in a circle or at a group table. Have the first child blow one note. Then ask the group to repeat that note. Encourage the child to discuss the locations of the paper sliders and demonstrate the breath they used so that everyone can imitate the note.

Next, ask the second child to blow a note. Again encourage the other children to imitate that note. Then ask the children to play the two notes together. Continue around the group table, adding notes to make a melody.

Variations:

- To increase the challenge, make the melody longer and ask the children to repeat it in unison.

- For cognitively impaired children have them blow to the tune of the "ABC."

CHAPTER 10

Success Stories

Classroom 205

Room 205 was chaotic. Most of the students were in their early teens, non-verbal, and spent most of the day focusing on life skills. Communication was limited to pointing, leading, reaching, sign approximations, and gestures. A broken voice output device and two tattered picture-exchange binders were on the top shelf of the cupboard, "out of harm's way."

My challenge was to teach each student how to use a communication system. Targeting communication goals on an individual basis for each student had been the focus of therapy for many years. The occupational therapist and I decided to teach communication as a whole-class effort.

We began with simple picture exchange of only the most highly motivating items and built student skills to include social pragmatics, sign language, picture exchange, voice output, and voicing to convey wants and needs. Some students became so successful that they were able to help set up and run The Store activities.

All the students reached their communication potential and are now able to use multi-modality communication to express themselves. Today, they sit at their desks, raise their hands, and wait in line for their turn. In less than six months all the students had completed all activities of The Store and the classroom staff was able to successfully maintain communication skills throughout the day. Classroom 205 is now a model classroom for communication. Way to go, Room 205!

Oral motor success story

This story begins with a group of young students with autism. Each student had challenges with coordination, blowing, sucking, chewing, bolus control, and low awareness of oral structures. I began an oral motor group that included all the students at every level in the hope that they would observe and learn from each other's strengths.

The first oral motor group was challenging for me. Toys and water were everywhere and I did not hear one single whistle or horn. I knew from past experiences that new groups take a while to assimilate into the daily routines.

By week two I was more prepared and had a plan. I put more responsibility on the students for gathering their supplies, getting them out of the bag, and putting them back when done. Also, I added a practice routine that included ten repetitions per blow toy, whistle, balloon, or horn. This worked. I actually heard whistles, horns, and saw some air go into balloons.

Today, we spend about 20 minutes on blowing/sucking and coordination activities, then play some music with wind "instruments," and end the group with sucking apple sauce through a straw or a frozen juice pop.

All of the young students can now blow, suck, chew, and have a better awareness of their oral abilities. This translates into better, safer, and neater meal times and builds a foundation for speech production. Way to go, Oral Motor group!

Artistry success story

I went to visit my aunt's house because I was invited to a get-together there. I came into the house and found my cousins playing on the Nintendo® Wii and having a fun time challenging each other on the console. I saw my aunt cleaning out her art closet when she found a bag with lots of toilet-paper rolls she had saved for art activities.

Right away she took the toilet rolls to a table and began decorating them with paper and connecting them with string. The rolls turned into a Nordic sea serpent and she "flew" the snake through the air into the room where the boys were playing their video game.

Immediately the boys asked, "What's that?" and exclaimed, "I want one of those." I got together with my cousins and helped them make a serpent like the one my aunt had made. Some of my cousins made serpents, others made Chinese dragons, and others yet made Falcor from "The Never Ending Story."

Their imaginations went wild and they kept adding different elements to the toilet rolls to make them ever so intricate. They were deep into the activity and they forgot all about their video game. In this day and age we have to struggle to get kids off the computer or their video game consoles, but this simple little activity had them enthralled. I was so happy to see how my aunt's simple art project beat out the newest video game on the market.

CONCLUSION

We have used these activities with both large and small groups, and on an individual basis. All the activities can be adjusted to meet the needs of individuals at every ability and age level. We have made them so that if your child has any siblings you can do the activity with the variation for your child's special needs, and then pick a different variation for the more advanced child or older sibling. This means that they can work on the same activity side by side but at their own level. It creates a bonding experience when the child who had normally felt different now feels that they can join in with their siblings. Another important factor to consider is the fact that children learn through modeling and parallel play. If both your children are playing the same game or working on the same activity (but one is working with the variation for their cognitive level) then the chances for learning through parallel play increase. And another great benefit of the variations is that the whole family can enjoy the same activity, making family game night or group activity time into a shared experience, rather than having isolated activities for different children in your household or classroom.

Teachers can do these activities in regular-education classrooms with higher functioning variations, and the mainstreamed kids who are still in a special education program can participate at their level without feeling the stigma of hearing, "This activity is too hard for you Johnny. Wait a minute and I'll give you something easier." Now they can all do the same activity.

Our book holds invaluable lessons that infuse many different aspects of learning, so that the entire brain can be activated at once. This provides a richer learning experience, one that can be remembered more easily because so many different parts of the brain are used to do the activity. By engaging all the senses we can provide the brain with a lot of feedback, and the mind will light up with electrical signaling from one part of the brain to the other. We want this holistic approach to learning because it sets forth a precedent for whole-brain learning. We want to build connections between different parts of the brain, and the best way to do this is through activities which use many parts of the mind at the same time. No more teaching in isolation. That was the past. Now we teach many parts of the brain at once. It is a new way of looking and thinking about the brain, and one that can bring us a lot of wonderful rewards.

We hope that this book is easy to use and easy to follow, so that you may have another quick and easily accessible tool to help you at your fingertips.

We have had significant success using the concepts, strategies, and best practices built into each activity and it is our sincerest hope that you will too. We strive to give children of all ages and capacities the tools they need to become more independent and feel better about themselves. We hope that parents can feel the pride that comes from learning that their children can now sort socks on their own, cook themselves a meal, tie their own shoes, and put on their own clothes. As adults we always want to feel like we are needed, but we also have to understand that if our children no longer need us then we have done a great job of raising them and teaching them the skills they need for this journey called life.

APPENDIX

Descriptors for the five senses

Sight

red	yellow	blue	green	white	black
bright	dark	dull	light	clear	transparent
shiny	shimmery	sparkly	pale	spotted	wrinkled
wide	narrow	pretty	ugly	crinkled	striped
clear	glowing	large	small	huge	tiny
massive	tall	short	fat	skinny	clean
dirty	robust	old	new	fragile	beautiful
pretty	ugly	used	handsome	slim	worn

Smell

perfumed	earthy	rose	dirty	moldy	flowery
sweet	stinky	pungent	spicy	skunky	reek
piney	fresh	tempting	sour	sharp	savory
scented	aromatic	fishy	clean	woody	rotten

Taste

good	sugary	tasteless	tangy	buttery	sweet
salty	spicy	burnt	bitter	sour	mellow
bland	fruity	peppery	oily	fishy	zesty

Touch

smooth	rough	dry	damp	wet	slimy
moist	scaly	fuzzy	silky	cold	hot
slippery	bumpy	warm	coarse	prickly	hard
soft	hairy	spiky	greasy	sharp	freezing
fluffy	grooved	rutted	scratchy	cool	textured

Sound

ring	cheer	loud	quiet	bang	pop
noisy	beat	whisper	yell	swish	ring
smash	bump	splash	bark	chirp	snap
yelp	shout	wheezy	honk	silent	snort
rumble	silent	hiss	whistle	crunch	sigh
clap	tap	rip	crack	tinkle	thud
hum	purr	buzz	chime	slam	screech
bang	thump	clap	stomp	racket	chortle
roar	shout	boom	scream	rhythmic	scratchy

Girl outline

SPEAK, MOVE, PLAY AND LEARN WITH CHILDREN ON THE AUTISM SPECTRUM

Boy outline

REFERENCES AND FURTHER READING

References

American Occupational Therapy Association (2008) "Occupational therapy practice framework: Domain and process." (2nd edition) *American Journal of Occupational Therapy 62*, 6, 625–683.

Ayres, A.J. (1972) "Improving academic scores through sensory integration." *Journal of Learning Disabilities 5*, 23–28.

Ayres, A.J. (1979) *Sensory Integration and the Child.* Los Angeles, CA: Western Psychological Services.

Barnes, K.J., Schoenfeld, H.G. and Pierson, W.P. (1997) "Inclusive schools: Implications for public school occupational therapy." *Physical Disabilities: Education and Related Services 15*, 2, 37–52.

Bazyk, S., Michaud, P., Goodman, G., Papp, P., Hawkins, E. and Welch, M.A. (2009) "Integrating occupational therapy services in a kindergarten curriculum: A look at the outcomes." *American Journal of Occupational Therapy 63*, 2, 160–171.

Bose, P. and Hinojosa, J. (2008) "Reported experiences from occupational therapists interacting with teachers in inclusive early childhood classrooms." *Journal of Occupational Therapy 62*, 3, 289–297.

Bowen, C. (2001) "Semantic and pragmatic difficulties and semantic pragmatic language disorder." Available at www.speech-language-therapy.com/spld.htm, accessed on 16 September 2009.

Briesmeister, J.M. and Schaefer, C.E. (eds) (1998) *Handbook of Parent Training: Parents as Co-therapists for Children's Behavior Problems.* Hoboken, NJ: John Wiley & Sons.

Capo, L.C. (2001) "Autism, employment, and the role of occupational therapy." *Work 16*, 3, 201–207.

Case-Smith, J. and Cable, J. (1996) "Perceptions of occupational therapists regarding service delivery models in school-based practice." *Occupational Therapy Journal of Research 16*, 1, 23–43.

Cermak, S.A., Stein, F. and Abelson, C. (1973) "Hyperactive children and an activity group therapy model." *The American Journal of Occupational Therapy 26*, 6, 311–315.

Degrace, B.W. (2004) "The everyday occupation of families with children with autism." *American Journal of Occupational Therapy 58*, 5, 543–550.

Dunn, W. (1982) "Independence through activity: The practice of occupational therapy (pediatrics)." *American Journal of Occupational Therapy 36*, 11, 745–748.

Karlstad, M. (1986) "Art in a first grade classroom." *Insights 19*, 2, 3–9.

Kielhofner, G. (1992) *Conceptual Foundation of Occupational Therapy.* Philadelphia, PA: F.A. Davis.

Ma, H., Trombly, C.A. and Robinson-Podolski, C. (1999) "The effects of context on skill acquisition and transfer." *Journal of Occupational Therapy 53*, 2, 138–144.

McCabe, A., Bliss, L., Barra, G. and Bennett, M.B. (2008) "Comparison of personal versus fictional narratives of children with language impairments." *American Journal of Speech-Language Pathology 17*, 194–206.

Mumford, M.S. (1974) "Verbal and activity groups." *American Journal of Occupational Therapy 28*, 5, 281–283.

Nevin, A.I. (2000) "Collaborating to Connect the Inclusion Puzzle." In R.A. Villa and J.S. Thousand (eds) *Restructuring for Caring and Effective Education: Piecing the Puzzle Together.* Baltimore, MD: Paul H. Brookes.

Nord, L.J. (1973) "An interdisciplinary educational program." *American Journal of Occupational Therapy 27*, 7, 404–412.

Sands, D., Kozleski, E. and French, N. (2000) *Inclusive Education for the 21st Century.* Belmont, CA: Wadsworth.

Technology-Related Assistance for Individuals with Disabilities Act of 1998, x USC § 100–407 (1998).

Watling, R., Deitz, J., Kanny, E.M. and McLaughlin, J.F. (1999) "Current practice of occupational therapy for children with autism." *Journal of Occupational Therapy 53*, 5, 498–505.

Whipple, J. (2004) "Music in intervention for children and adolescents with Autism: A meta-analysis." *Journal of Music Therapy 41*, 2, 90–106.

Further reading

American Speech-Language-Hearing Association (ASHA) (2011) "Social language use (Pragmatics)." Available at www.asha.org/public/speech/development/pragmatics.htm, accessed on 20 February 2011.

Ashburner, J., Ziviani, J. and Rodger, S. (2008) "Sensory processing and classroom emotional, behavioral, and educational outcomes in children with autism spectrum disorder." *American Journal of Occupational Therapy 62*, 5, 564–573.

Ayres, A.J. (1972) *Sensory Integration and Learning Disorders.* Los Angeles, CA: Western Psychological Services.

Bondy, A.S. (2001) "PECS: Potential benefits and risks." *The Behavior Analyst Today 2*, 127–132.

Bondy, A.S. and Frost, L. (1994) "The Picture Exchange Communication System." *Focus on Autistic Behavior 9*, 3, 1–19.

Bondy, A.S. and Frost, L. (2001) "The Picture Exchange Communication System." *Behavior Modification 25*, 5, 725–744.

Bundy, A., Lane, S. and Murray, E. (2002) *Sensory Integration Theory and Practice* (2nd edition). Philadelphia, PA: F.A. Davis.

Case-Smith, J. and Bryan, T. (1999) "The effects of occupational therapy with sensory integration emphasis on preschool age children with autism." *American Journal of Occupational Therapy 53*, 5, 489–497.

Charlop-Christy, M.H., Carpenter, M., Le, L., LeBlanc, L.A. and Kellet, K. (2002) "Using the Picture Exchange Communication System (PECS) with children with autism: Assessment of PECS acquisition, speech, social-communicative behavior, and problem behavior." *Journal of Applied Behavior Analysis 35*, 3, 213–231.

Ganz, J.B. and Simpson, R.L. (2004) "Effects on communicative requesting and speech development of the Picture Exchange Communication System in children with characteristics of autism." *Journal of Autism and Developmental Disorders 34*, 4, 395–409.

Hanft, B.E., Miller, L.J. and Lane, S.J. (2000) "Towards a consensus in terminology in sensory integration theory and practice: Part 3. Observable behaviors: Sensory integration dysfunction." *Sensory Integration Special Interest Quarterly 23*, 3, 93–96.

Harris, E. (2008) "The meanings of craft to an occupational therapist." *Australian Occupational Therapy Journal 55*, 133–142.

Hofmann, A.O. (2009) "Supporting parents of children with autism: The role of occupational therapy." Available at www.aota.org/Consumers/professionals/WhatisOT/CY/Articles/41229.aspx, accessed on October 30, 2011.

Howlin, P., Gordon, R.K., Pasco, G., Wade, A. and Charman, T. (2007) "The effectiveness of Picture Exchange Communication System (PECS) training for teachers of children with autism: A pragmatic, group randomised controlled trial." *Journal of Child Psychology and Psychiatry 48*, 5, 473–481.

Lane, S.J., Miller, L.J. and Hanft, B.E. (2000) "Towards a consensus in terminology in sensory integration theory and practice: Part 2. Sensory integration patterns of function and dysfunction." *Sensory Integration Special Interest Quarterly 23*, 2, 90–92.

Mauer, D.M. (1999) "Issues and applications of sensory integration theory and treatment with children with language disorders." *Language, Speech, and Hearing Services in Schools 30*, 383–392.

Miller, L.J. and Lane, S.J. (2000) "Towards a consensus in terminology in sensory integration theory and practice: Part 1: Taxonomy of neurophysiological processes." *Sensory Integration Special Interest Quarterly 23*, 1–4.

Mirenda, P. (2001) "Autism, augmentative communication, and assistive technology: What do we really know?" *Focus on Autism and Other Developmental Disabilities 16*, 3, 141–151.

Schwartz, I.S., Garfinkle, A.N. and Bauer, J. (1998) "The Picture Exchange Communication System: Communicative outcomes for young children with disabilities." *Topics in Early Childhood Special Education 18*, 3, 144–159.

Velde, B.P. (1999) "The Language of Crafts." In G.S. Fidler and B.P.Velde (eds) *Activities: Reality and Symbol*. Thorofare, NJ: Slack.

Windeck, S.L. and Laurel, M.L. (1989) "Sensory integration: A theoretical framework combining speech-language therapy with sensory integration treatment." *Sensory Integration Special Interest Section Quarterly 12*, 1, 84–88.

Yoder, P. and Stone, W.L. (2006) "A randomized comparison of the effect of two prelinguistic communication interventions on the acquisition of spoken communication in preschoolers with ASD." *Journal of Speech, Language, and Hearing Research 49*, 4, 698–711.